W9-ACA-794

DOES WRITING HAVE A FUTURE?

Electronic Mediations

Katherine Hayles, Mark Poster,
and Samuel Weber, Series Editors

(continued on page 180)

Does Writing Have a Future?

Vilém Flusser

Introduction by Mark Poster
Translated by Nancy Ann Roth

Electronic Mediations
VOLUME 33

University of Minnesota Press
MINNEAPOLIS · LONDON

Originally published as *Die Schrift. Hat Schreiben Zukunft?*
Copyright 1987 European Photography, Andreas Müller-
Pohle, P. O. Box 08 02 27, D-10002 Berlin, Germany, www.
equivalence.com. Edition Flusser, Volume V (2002⁵).

Published by the University of Minnesota Press
111 Third Avenue South, Suite 290
Minneapolis, MN 55401-2520
http://www.upress.umn.edu

Library of Congress Cataloging-in-Publication Data

Flusser, Vilém, 1920–1991.
 [Schrift. English]
 Does writing have a future? / Vilém Flusser ; introduction by
Mark Poster ; translated by Nancy Ann Roth.
   p. cm. — (Electronic mediations ; v. 33)
Includes bibliographical references and index.
 ISBN 978-0-8166-7022-2 (hc : alk. paper)
 ISBN 978-0-8166-7023-9 (pb : alk. paper)
1. Writing—Philosophy. 2. Written communication. I. Poster,
Mark. II. Title.
 P211.F68 2011
 302.2'244—dc22
                    2010030719

17 16 15 14 13 12 11   10 9 8 7 6 5 4 3 2 1

For Abraham Moles,
who discovered and began to research writing
after writing.

Contents

Does Writing Have a Future?

An Introduction to Vilém Flusser's *Into the Universe of Technical Images* and *Does Writing Have a Future?*

Mark Poster

Vilém Flusser remains relatively unknown to readers of critical theory, cultural studies, and media studies, particularly among readers of English. Given this, the Electronic Mediations series of the University of Minnesota Press herewith publishes in English translation two of his most important works, *Does Writing Have a Future?* and *Into the Universe of Technical Images,* both translated by Nancy Ann Roth. We trust that these publications, in addition to those already available from this and other presses, will bring Flusser's ideas to a wider English audience. Flusser ought not to require an introduction such as I provide because his work is crucial to a world saturated by a culture highly dependent on media. The production, reproduction, consumption, dissemination, and storage of texts, images, and sounds increasingly rely on electronic devices, almost always nowadays in a digital format. The immense implication of the dramatic spread of media in everyday life is beginning to dawn on most of us. Yet much remains to be done in theorizing information media and studying it empirically.

Many obstacles stand in the way of fresh thinking about media. Media are surely central to Western societies of the past several centuries and to the emerging global societies of the contemporary era and the future. There is a thickening, intensification, and increasing complexity to the use of information machines, technologies that are necessary in the production, reproduction, storage, and distribution of texts, images, and sounds—the constituent elements of culture. This phenomenon has been termed a "media ecology,"[1] adding a new layer to the ecologies of animal, vegetable, and mineral. It behooves anyone engaged in critical discourse to take serious account of media. I argue that media offer a key to understanding the process of globalization in relation to a new configuration of interaction between humans and machines.

Media are not easy to define, and one's approach to them affects considerably the character and limits of one's discourse. All too often, media are generalized and made transcendent, as in the characteristic gesture of Western theory in which humans are tool-making animals, enjoying the benefits of their tools "for the relief of man's estate," as Francis Bacon put it a half millennium ago.[2] Descartes provided the metaphysics to Bacon's utopian imaginings: humans are spirit, subjects for whom material workings, including of the human body, comprise little more than inert matter to be shaped and fashioned for human betterment. This ontology oscillates between praising the freedom of the human mind and cringing with anxiety at the possibility of its diminution should these external objects rise up and threaten it. The name for this threat is *technological determinism,* so poignantly portrayed by Charlie Chaplin in the film *Modern Times.*

Another problematic aspect of the Western figure of the tool-making animal is the confounding of media with technology. Machines that process texts, images, and sounds, I contend, are significantly distinct from machines that act on materials like wood and iron. However important these mechanical machines are, they are very different and have very different implications from information machines. Media machines act on the components of culture, not nature (if that distinction may still be employed), affecting human beings in a way very different from mechanical machines. One might say that information machines are closer to humans than mechanical machines and establish relations with them that are more profound.

It is urgent to rid critical discourse of the older framework of tool-making creatures and seek openings to the comprehension of the relation of humans to information machines, openings that promise alternatives to the binary of freedom and determinism. Such frameworks would need to acknowledge the logics of both the human and the machine as well as the logics of their various and multiple interactions. They would account for the interface between the two as well as the extension of their interactions across the planet, often violating political and cultural boundaries and forming new domains of politics and culture. These are the weighty issues raised by the simple term *media.* One theorist who braved these paths was Vilém Flusser.

Vilém Flusser can be compared to Marshall McLuhan and Jean Baudrillard. Similar to McLuhan, Flusser takes media seriously, and as does Baudrillard, he discerns the impact of media on culture. Like both McLuhan and Baudrillard, Flusser theorized media culture well before many other cultural theorists thought seriously about it. (There are certainly some notable exceptions: Walter Benjamin, Harold Innis, and Hans Magnus Enzensberger come immediately to mind.) Michel Foucault, Jacques Lacan, Louis Althusser, Jean-François Lyotard, Jürgen Habermas, Ernesto Laclau, Homi K. Bhabha, and Judith Butler—the list could be extended considerably of major theorists from the 1970s onward who either paid no attention at all to the vast changes in media culture taking place under their noses or who commented on the media only as a tool that amplified other institutions like capitalism or representative democracy. Against this group of thinkers, Flusser stands out, with only a handful of others, as one who presciently and insightfully deciphered the codes of materiality disseminated under the apparatuses of the media.

Perhaps one reason for the relative lack of attention to media by cultural theorists was the polemical antics of McLuhan, Baudrillard, and Flusser. The Canadian, the Frenchman, and the Czech all reveled in poking fun at those who failed to see the importance of media. Like McLuhan, Flusser repeatedly hailed the end of print and the onset of the age of images. He opens his book on writing, for example, with the following: "Writing, in the sense of placing letters and other marks one after another, appears to have little or no future."[3] Just as McLuhan pronounced the end of the "Gutenberg Galaxy," so Flusser proclaimed the end of writing. Neither would appeal much to a theoretical world that was discovering the importance of language, writing, and so forth. And in a mental habitus of scorn for popular culture, all three took seriously the importance of television (McLuhan), style (Baudrillard), and popularizing and extending symbolic exchanges on the global network (Flusser). One might say the importance of their work rests not so much with their insight into the phenomena of electronic media but with the simple and more basic fact that they paid attention to it at all.

Characteristic criticism of Flusser is found in an essay by Friedrich Kittler. Kittler objects to the sharp distinction drawn by McLuhan and Flusser between print and images:

> Media theorists, specifically Marshall McLuhan and, succeeding him, Vilem Flusser, draw an absolute distinction between writing and the image that ultimately rests on concepts of geometry. They contrast the linearity or one-dimensionality of printed books with the irreducible two-dimensionality of images. Simplified in this manner, it is a distinction that may hold true even when computer technology can model texts as strings, as it does today. But it suppresses the simple facts emphasized long ago and, not coincidentally, by a *nouveau romancier,* Michel Butor: the books used most often—the Bible, once upon a time, and today more likely the telephone book—are certainly not read in a linear manner.[4]

Kittler's critique of the binary print–image serves a cautionary role against overgeneralization but does not grapple with the basic issue of media specificity and its cultural implications. His critique is somewhat puzzling given his Foucauldian, historical approach to media, in which "discourse networks" are defined by epochs and are accordingly decidedly different from one another.[5]

One area of Flusser's media theory that deserves special attention is the connection he drew between writing and history and the implications of this analysis for a concept of temporality. In his discussions of media and history, Flusser—one might say without exaggeration—denaturalizes temporality with a systematicity not seen perhaps since Vico.[6] Flusser first argues that history is not possible without writing:

> With the invention of writing, history begins, not because writing keeps a firm hold on processes, but because it transforms scenes into processes: it generates historical consciousness.[7]

In the relation Flusser draws between writing and history, media practice already plays a central role in culture, in this case, as the awareness of time as linear movement. But already for him, "writing" performs the function of changing "scenes into processes." Thereby Flusser contrasts culture based on writing with culture based on images. In contrast to Derrida, Flusser associates the institution of writing not so much with a change in the form of memory (as *différance*) but with resistance to images: "Greek philosophy and Jewish prophecy are battle cries against images on behalf of texts."[8] Whereas for Derrida, the ancient Greeks at least focused on the danger of writing in comparison to speech, Flusser's binary of writing and images yields a different conclusion regarding the Greek valuation of writing.

What becomes most salient for Flusser's theory of media is the consequence of writing for temporality. Flusser makes a great deal of the fact that writing is linear—that in this medium, one thing inexorably comes after another. One cannot easily skip around in a written text (i.e., until hypertext emerged with the digitization of writing). Try as they might, theorists such as Roland Barthes and writers from Laurence Sterne to Raymond Quéneau and the Oulipo group have at best great difficulty in constructing texts that allow or encourage the reader to find her own way through the page.[9] Flusser's insistence on the linearity of writing, despite these exceptions and demurrals, is convincing. He writes,

> Linear codes demand a synchronization of their diachronicity. They demand progressive reception. And the result is a new experience of time, that is, linear time, a stream of unstoppable progress, of dramatic unrepeatability, of framing, in short, history.[10]

It might be noted that for the most part, historians have traditionally sided with Flusser on the question of the relation of history to writing but not usually for the same reasons. Historians claim that without writing, there is no material, objective basis for memory about the past; as Flusser says, writing keeps "a firm hold on the past." Put differently, Flusser distinguishes his argument regarding the relation of writing to history from the argument of historians as follows:

> The difference between prehistory and history is not that we have written documents . . . , but that during history there are literate men who experience, understand, and evaluate the world as a "becoming."[11]

Societies without writing are thereby societies without history. Historians' penchant for the fullness of the written text, and the face value of truth contained therein, is, of course, not Flusser's claim. Not perhaps until the second half of the twentieth century, with studies of the Holocaust[12] and other traumatic experiences more generally, have historians reconsidered the unique value of writing for their discipline, opening up the possibility that historical research might find evidentiary truth in oral reports and by conducting interviews. Also, influenced by anthropological and archeological methods, some historians consider material artifacts, objects without writing, at least as a supplementary source for their archives.

But Flusser's argument for the relation of writing to temporality has not been a major focus of historians. Flusser stresses the unidirectional flow of writing as well as its "unrepeatability" as prominent aspects of this medium, aspects that militate, if not determine, a cultural inscription of time as progressive. For Flusser, practices of writing and reading induce a linear sense of time and give prominence to diachronicity in general as compared with synchronicity. For Flusser, modern society's break with the general human sense of time as cyclical, an obvious extrapolation from nature's rhythms, owes a deep debt to the increasing salience of writing over the past several centuries. The full extension of time as a linear progression emerged not with the simple discovery of writing but with a number of social and cultural changes commensurate with modern society: the printing press that made writing widely reproducible, the spread of compulsory education in modern democracies, the rise of urban commercial cultures with their heavy reliance on written documents, the emergence of the modern state with its bureaucratic form, and so forth.

There is another facet to Flusser's theory of writing and temporality that deserves mention. For Flusser, writing as a medium encourages a specific form of temporality. The medium and the character of time are particular. This suggests that each medium might have an associated, special form of temporality. Flusser's media theory thereby accounts for the specificity of each information technology. His view contrasts sharply with Derrida's view in the sense that the latter understands the temporal logic of writing as paradigmatic for all media—indeed, for all technology. As a result, deconstruction has difficulty distinguishing between media cultures such as between writing cultures and image cultures. Bernard Stiegler finds fault with Derrida on precisely these grounds,[13] with the consequence that the relation of media technology to time is very different in the views of Derrida and Flusser.

If history, for Flusser, is a linear mode of consciousness related to writing, today it must be considered in crisis. The reason for the crisis is simply that writing is being supplanted by images—a new medium is being added to the old and taking priority over it in the culture. Flusser understands this change in media in several ways. From a historical point of view (and there is some degree of irony in Flusser's reliance on history for periodizing media changes), image culture begins with the photograph.[14] As technically produced images, photographs encourage a nonlinear form of composition and reading. They "are dams placed in the way of the stream of history, jamming historical happenings."[15] The temporality of reading photographs is an all-at-onceness, not a linear progression. Written texts are decoded in a linear fashion, in a sequence of steps that are narrative in nature, moving from start to finish. According to Flusser, the process of interpreting images is different: "In pictures we may get the message first, and then try to decompose it. . . . This difference is one of temporality, and involved the present, the past and the future."[16] The "historical time" of the written text induces a directional sense in the reader, a feeling of going somewhere, whereas images are read with no sense of movement, with a feeling of going nowhere.

In their composition, as well, Flusser regards photographs as different from writing because they rely on a "calculating, formal" type of thinking.[17] Yet for him, photographs are not a throwback to prehistoric times. There is no identity between photographs and cave paintings, for instance. The latter are mimetic, whereas photographs "are computed possibilities (models, projections onto the environment)."[18]

Flusser is perhaps least convincing in his insistence on the difference between prehistoric images and photographs. Even if photographs have the formal property of "models," one might say the same about cave paintings. And even if cave paintings are in the first instance mimetic, one might easily argue that photographs, at least until the advent of digital technology, have had a mimetic quality as well. Certainly in the culture at large of the nineteenth century, photographs were in good part regarded as indexical. To make Flusser's argument more convincing, one might analyze the difference between the technology of prehistoric images and photography. The difference in the composition process between the two forms of image production is certainly stark. A close reading of *Into the Universe of Technical Images* might help to clarify the distinction for the reader.

In his analysis of the different temporalities of writing and images, Flusser develops a theory of the visual. Writing and images are as different as lines and surfaces. The former, as we have seen, produces historical society, the latter "telematic society." Flusser describes this new world as follows: "The telematic society would be the first to recognize the production of information as society's actual function, and so to systematically foster this production: the first self-conscious and therefore free society."[19] In a somewhat utopian vein, Flusser foresees revolutionary changes when digital images replace first text and then analog images (television, photography, cinema). He imagines, as well, the end of the reign of the author, very much like Foucault and Barthes. He writes, "For genuinely disciplined, theorized creativity will only be possible after the myth of the author of information is abandoned."[20] For Flusser, computer-generated images require a level of creativity unknown in the past, when copying nature was the goal of image production.

The cultural study of media is hampered by a philosophical tradition based on the *episteme* of the transcendental, unconditional, and contextless "I think." From Kant (time as a synthetic a priori of reason) to Husserl (time as a feature of consciousness as it appears to thought) and even to Bergson (time as duration), the nature of time is deduced from logic. A change comes with Derrida and the association of time with the technology of writing, but here again, writing becomes a form (*différance*) inherent to all media and thereby divorced from technological specificity and social practice. Stiegler, in his three-volume work *Technics and Time,* attempts to break from this tradition by inserting technology more firmly within the conceptual formation of time. In his essay "Derrida and Technology" as well as in his televised debate with Derrida, published as a transcripted book titled *Echographies,* Stiegler complains that when Derrida theorizes writing as "arche-writing," he places technology in a register of temporality that loses the specificity of different media: "All [media for Derrida]," he writes, "are figures . . . of origin that arche-writing constitutes."[21] Time is thus possible for Stiegler (as for Flusser) through the technical inscription of cultural objects. Wrestling with the question of the transcendental nature of media temporality, Stiegler concludes on a middle ground of what he calls "a-transcendentality."[22]

In Mark Hansen's review of volume 1 of *Technics and Time,* he points out that Stiegler's discovery of the discreteness of the digital image leads him to posit media as constituting subjects in different forms of the awareness of time.[23] Photography, film, and networked computing thus construct distinctly different forms of temporality in the subject. Yet Stiegler, rigorous and systematic in his thinking, still maintains a kind of original disposition of media as material forms of memory, as prostheses. The question that remains open in his work, and that provides a fruitful intersection with Flusser's media theory, is the degree of determination one would give to this primary or initial prosthetic figure. I argue that one must theorize time and media in such a way that the relation is not entirely dependent on the human as ground but instead opens a more complex possibility for multiple assemblages of the human and the machine, not as prostheses *for* the human but as mixtures of human–machine in which the outcome or specific forms of the relation are not prefigured in the initial conceptualization of the relation. Contingency of the relation must be kept open. In that way, the different cultural forms of media and time would each have their own validity, and the critical question of how to institute the newer relation in networked computing would remain an open political question.

Given the importance of the question of media, and of Flusser's work in this area, it is disappointing that the major cultural theorists of the 1970s and 1980s tend to overlook media theory and almost completely ignore the thought of Flusser. Let us take a brief glance at some examples of this lack and this problem.

Michel Foucault provides an interesting example of the problem that also persists in Derrida's work, as we have seen. Foucault's work of the 1970s is densely sprinkled with metaphors of media. *Discipline and Punish* and *The History of Sexuality, Volume 1,* centrally rely on such figures as "technology of power" and "networks," in which individuals are understood as "nodes." His understanding of the individual or subject as constituted by and living within networks in everyday life is highly suggestive for an understanding of the role of media. Similarly, his depiction of the confessional as a peculiar space of speech in early modern France moves very close to an analysis of one form of language in relation to subject positions. Even more, his enigmatic depiction of a world beyond the author function suggests the types of exchanges that prevailed on the Internet before the phenomenon of global communication actually existed:

> All discourses . . . would then develop in the anonymity of a murmur. We would no longer hear the questions that have been rehashed for so long: Who really spoke? Is it really he and not someone else? With what authenticity or original-ity? And what part of his deepest self did he express in his discourse? Instead there would be other questions, like these:

What are the modes of existence of this discourse? Where has it been used, how can it circulate, and who can appropriate it for himself? What are the places in it where there is room for possible subjects? Who can assume these various subject functions? And behind all these questions, we would hear hardly anything but the stirring of an indifference: What difference does it make who is speaking?[24]

Here Foucault seems to anticipate the world of chat rooms, e-mail, blogs, and Web pages, where authorship is always in question. He seems to depict, and even desire, a space of communication where identity may be in doubt and subordinated to the flow of text, to the impulses of creativity. And yet the word *media* is absent from the vocabulary of the critic of authorship. In the end, however, aside from passing comments on the importance of writing in the care of self, Foucault does not theorize media as a significant domain of what he calls "subjectivation."

Then there is Jacques Lacan, whose work has stimulated the important writings of Slavoj Žižek but whose own work on media provides perhaps the most egregious examples of the problem I am addressing. In his widely read (and viewed) television interview purportedly about television and published in transcript form as *Television,* Lacan demonstrates quite clearly that he has, I am sorry to report, not a whiff of understanding about media. Complaining that the rebellious Parisian students of May 1968 were acting without a shred of guilt or shame, Lacan argues in *Seminar XVII* that the young people have symbolically slain their parents because they have failed to recognize the authority of the gaze of the Other. Thus they cannot come under the Law, or become subjects of desire through the good graces of the master signifier, and so on. The important point in this stunning application of psychoanalysis to media is that Lacan attributes this moral transgression to television. Why? Because with television, there is a voice but no individual.[25] The obvious question is, how is television different from radio, film, or the Internet, which also emit voices without the speaker's presence? Indeed, books, newspapers—all forms of print—might be included in the list, although in these cases, "voice" is not accompanied by sound. Why, then, limit the complaint to television? Clearly media studies will not be well informed by psychoanalysis if Lacan is any guide.[26]

Gilles Deleuze provides another variation of the absence of media in twentieth-century theory. The seminal, even magisterial works he composed with Félix Guattari, *Anti-Oedipus* and *A Thousand Plateaus,* explore critically the social and cultural space of modernity without mention of media. Their absence threatens to undermine what is otherwise a compelling rethinking of Western reality. The same may be said of Deleuze's two volumes on film.[27] The one exception within Deleuze's considerable and weighty corpus is the short essay "Postscript on Control Societies" (1990),[28] whose title suggests its marginal position in his thought. In the English-speaking discursive community, thinkers have so yearned for a discussion of media that this slight piece has gained attention and praise far exceeding its modest standing. Because of its celebrity, if for no other reason, it is worthy of attention.

In this brief piece, Deleuze emphasizes the absence of confining spatial arrangements in the exercise of domination afforded by the use of computer technology. "What has changed," in the formulation of Deleuze's argument by Hardt and Negri, "is that, along with the collapse of the institutions, the disciplinary *dispositifs* have become less limited and bounded spatially in the social field. Carceral discipline, school discipline, factory discipline, and so forth interweave in a hybrid production of subjectivity."[29] Beyond the negative trait of the absence of "major organizing sites of confinement,"[30] control societies are, in this text, maddeningly undefined. Deleuze discusses the control society again in "Having an Idea in Cinema"[31] but is again both brief and vague, only adding to his previous discussion that because "information is precisely the system of control,"[32] "counterinformation" becomes a form of resistance,[33] all of which suggests to me that Deleuze's understanding of networked digital information machines remains rudimentary. It is hard to imagine what counterinformation might be, for example. Does he mean that critical content is resistance? Or does the form of the critical content constitute resistance?

It might seem logical to conclude from the opposition between societies of discipline and societies of control that Deleuze places himself against Foucault, or at least that he is going beyond Foucault by discerning forms of domination unthought by the historian of the Panopticon. Yet such is not at all the case. Instead, Deleuze proclaims his agreement with Foucault, citing William Burroughs again as the fulcrum of the matter. Deleuze writes, "Foucault agrees with Burroughs who claims that our future will be controlled rather than disciplined."[34] But Deleuze gives no evidence that Foucault anticipated a transformation to societies of control, relegating discipline to the garbage can of history. It would appear that Deleuze was unwilling to position himself as the thinker who went beyond Foucault even as, in the same paragraph, Deleuze compellingly characterizes the break between the two orders of domination. In the following passage, Deleuze insists that Foucault adopts the notion of societies of control: "The disciplines which Foucault describes are the history of what we gradually cease to be, and our present-day reality takes on the form of dispositions of overt and continuous *control* in a way which is very different from recent closed disciplines."[35]

Deleuze's stadial theory, moving from discipline to control, is also far too linear in character. Elements of control existed in Europe in the early modern period as the state hired spies to keep track of suspected miscreants. Equally, forms of discipline proliferate in the twenty-first century as the United States, for example, erects more and more prisons under the so-called get tough policies of recent and current administrations. The shift from discipline to control is also Eurocentric, overlooking the very different disposition of these state strategies in the southern hemisphere. François

Vergès points out, for example, that "in postcolonial Reunion, these two strategies have concurrently occurred. New types of sanction, education, and care have constructed a web of control around the Creoles, and along with the creation of a vast social network of control, there has been a multiplication of prisons, a criminalization and psychologization of politics."[36] Deleuze's model of control as the next stage after discipline thus contains problems at numerous levels.

In an essay from 1998, Michael Hardt attempts to explicate the concept of societies of control beyond what Deleuze has given us. He asserts that as the chief new form of power, "the metaphorical space of the societies of control is perhaps best characterized by the shifting desert sands, where positions are continually swept away; or better, the smooth surfaces of cyberspace, with its infinitely pro-grammable flows of codes and information."[37] Smooth surfaces are opposed to striated planes, categories one recalls from *A Thousand Plateaus*[38] that designate homogeneous and heterogeneous spaces, respectively.[39] But Hardt overlooks the side of cyberspace that resists the power formation of the control society, all kinds of spaces in which copyright law, fixed identities, censorship, and so forth, are continuously evaded and challenged. Cyberspace is hardly Hardt's smooth surface of transparency and control but is rather a highly differentiated field of resistance, conflict, and uncertainty.

For Hardt, control societies are "smooth" because civil society has collapsed, rendering the social lacking in mediations.[40] Hardt analyzes the dialectic of civil society from Hegel to Foucault, con-cluding that "what has come to an end, or more accurately declined in importance in post–civil society, then, are precisely these func-tions of mediation or education and the institutions that gave them form."[41] Foucault's disciplinary institutions have lost their ability to position and give identity to individuals. Replacing the spaces of confinement, according to Hardt, are the media. But again, one must object: the media are also mediating, albeit in a different form from older establishments like education and the family. What is lacking in Hardt's understanding of the move from discipline to control is precisely an analysis of media as technologies of power. Surely media are different from prisons, education, and so forth, but one must understand the specificity of media as structuring systems as well as pay attention to the differences of one medium from another. Television, print, and the Internet are each a disciplinary institution—in this sense, they are different from each other but also similar to prisons in that they construct subjects, define identities, position individuals, and configure cultural objects. True enough, media do not require spatial arrangements in the manner of workshops and prisons, but humans remain fixed in space and time: at the computer, in front of the television set, walking or bicycling through city streets, or riding on a subway with headphones and an MP3 player or cell phone. I refer to this configuration of the construction of the subject as a *superpanopticon* to indicate its difference from modern institutions.[42] The term *control society* bears the disadvantage of losing an ability to capture the new technologies of power: the media.

At a more general level, what stands in the way of an approach to media theory for Deleuze is his understanding of film as art. From *Difference and Repetition* to the cinema books of the 1980s, Deleuze frames cinema only as art. When he recognizes the altered sphere of everyday life as steeped in audio and visual technologies, he finds in art a liberatory escape from the quotidian: "The more our daily life appears standardized, stereotyped and subject to an accelerated reproduction of objects of consumption, the art must be injected into it."[43] One cannot come near the problem of media with a view of the everyday as degraded, debased, and baleful.

Perhaps a turn to Flusser will change the disregard for media that has so characterized cultural theory of the 1970s, 1980s, and 1990s. Flusser, however flamboyant and polemical his writing can be, thought deeply about the emergence of electronic media and their implications not only for Western culture but also truly for global culture.

Notes

1   Matthew Fuller, *Media Ecologies: Materialist Energies in Art and Technoculture* (Cambridge, Mass.: MIT Press, 2005).

2   Francis Bacon, *The Advancement of Learning* (London: Cassell, 1893), book 1, chap. 5, para. 11.

3   Vilém Flusser, *Writings* (Minneapolis: University of Minnesota Press, 2002), 1.

4   Friedrick Kittler, "Perspective and the Book," *Grey Room* 5 (2001): 39.

5   Friedrick Kittler, *Discourse Networks: 1800/1900* (Palo Alto, Calif.: Stanford University Press, 1990).

6   Giambattista Vico, *The New Science* (Ithaca, N.Y.: Cornell University Press, 1984).

7   Flusser, *Writings*, 39.

8   Ibid.

9   Katherine Hayles, *Writing Machines* (Cambridge, Mass.: MIT Press, 2002).

10 Ibid., 39.

11 Flusser, *Writings*, 63.

12 Dominick LaCapra, *History and Memory after Auschwitz* (Ithaca, N.Y.: Cornell University Press, 1988).

13 Jacques Derrida and Bernhard Stiegler, *Echographies de la télévision: entretiens filmés* (Paris: Institut national de l'autovisuel, 1996).

14 Vilém Flusser, *Towards a Philosophy of Photography* (Gottingen, Germany: European Photography, 1984).

15 Flusser, *Writings*, 127.

16 Ibid., 23.

17 Ibid., 128.

18 Ibid., 129.

19 Vilém Flusser, *Into the Universe of Technical Images* (Minneapolis: University of Minnesota Press, 2011), 92.

20 Ibid., 101.

21 Jacques Derrida and Bernhard Stiegler, *Echographies of Television* (London: Polity, 2002), 239.

22 B. Stiegler, "Our Ailing Institutions," *Culture Machine* XX (1993).

23 Mark Hansen, "'Realtime Synthesis' and the Différance of the Body: Technocultural Studies in the Wake of Deconstruction," *Culture Machine* XX (2004).

24 Michel Foucault, "What Is an Author?" in *The Foucault Reader*, ed. P. Rabinow (New York: Pantheon, 1984), 119–20.

25 Jacques Lacan, *Television* (New York: W. W. Norton, 1990), 27.

26 Sigmund Freud, *Civilization and Its Discontents* (New York: W. W. Norton, 1961), 39, also manifests a deep unconcern for media. In his famous example of the telephone, he quips that it provides no more satisfaction than sticking one's leg out from under the covers on a cold winter night just to be able to return it to comfort and warmth afterward. For a very different view of the value of Lacan's insights on television, see Rosalind Morris, "The War Drive: Image Files Corrupted," *Social Text* 25, no. 2 (2007): 103–42.

27 Gilles Deleuze, *Cinema 1: The Movement-Image* (Minneapolis: University of Minnesota Press, 1986).

28 Gilles Deleuze, "Postscript on Control Societies," in *Negotiations: 1972–1980* (New York: Columbia University Press, 1990), 177–82.

29 Michael Hardt and Antonio Negri, *Empire* (Cambridge, Mass.: Harvard University Press, 2000), 330.

30 Gilles Deleuze, *Negotiations: 1972–1990* (New York: Columbia University Press, 1995), 177.

31 Gilles Deleuze, "Having an Idea in Cinema," in *Deleuze and Guattari: New Mappings in Politics, Philosophy, and Culture*, ed. Eleanor Kaufman and Kevin Heller (Minneapolis: University of Minnesota Press, 1998), 14–19.

32 Ibid., 17.

33 Ibid., 18.

34 Gilles Deleuze, "What Is a *Dispositif?*" in *Michel Foucault Philosopher,* ed. François Ewald (New York: Routledge, 1992), 164.

35 Ibid.

36 François Vergès, *Monsters and Revolutionaries: Colonial Family Romance and Métissage* (Durham, N.C.: Duke University Press, 1999), 219.

37 Michael Hardt, "Withering of Civil Society," *Social Text* 45 (Winter 1995): 32.

38 Gilles Deleuze and Félix Guattari, *A Thousand Plateaus: Capitalism and Schizophrenia* (Minneapolis: University of Minnesota Press, 1987).

39 Ibid.

40 Hardt, "Withering of Civil Society."

41 Ibid., 36.

42 Mark Poster, *The Mode of Information: Poststructuralism and Social Context* (Chicago: University of Chicago Press, 1990).

43 Gilles Deleuze, *Difference and Repetition,* trans. Paul Patton (New York: Columbia University Press, 1994), 293.

DOES WRITING HAVE A FUTURE?

Introduction

Writing, in the sense of placing letters and other marks one after another, appears to have little or no future. Information is now more effectively transmitted by codes other than those of written signs. What was once written can now be conveyed more effectively on tapes, records, films, videotapes, videodisks, or computer disks, and a great deal that could not be written until now can be noted down in these new codes. Information coded by these means is easier to produce, to transmit, to receive, and to store than written texts. Future correspondence, science, politics, poetry, and philosophy will be pursued more effectively through the use of these codes than through the alphabet or Arabic numerals. It really looks as though written codes will be set aside, like Egyptian hieroglyphs or Indian knots. Only historians and other specialists will be obliged to learn reading and writing in the future.

Many people deny this, mainly out of laziness. They have already learned to write, and they are too old to learn the new codes. We surround this, our laziness, with an aura of grandeur and nobility. If we were to lose writing, we say, we would lose everything we owe to such people as Homer, Aristotle, and Goethe, to say nothing of the Holy Bible. Only how do we really know that these great writers, including the Author of the Bible, would not have preferred to speak into a microphone or to film?

But laziness doesn't explain everything. There are people, and I count myself among them, who believe that they could not live without writing. And this is not because they want to imitate Homer, for they know that no one can write as he did anymore, even a second

Homer; rather they believe that writing is a necessity because their being is expressed in, and only in, the gesture of writing.

Of course, they could be wrong. But even assuming that they are right and that the production of video clips does not suit their being, their *forma mentis,* it would not prove that their form of being has become obsolete, that such people have become dinosaurs. It's true that not everything obsolete is necessarily expendable. What is called progress is not necessarily the same thing as improvement. Dinosaurs were very nice animals in their way, after all. And yet the insistence on writing is becoming questionable today.

The question is, What is distinctive about writing? What sets it apart from comparable gestures of the past and future—from painting, from pressing on computer keys? Is there anything specific at all that is shared by all kinds of gestures of writing—from the chiseling of Latin letters in marble to the brushing of Chinese ideograms on silk, the scratching of equations on boards, or the pounding on the keys of typewriters? What sort of life did people have before they began to write? And how would their lives look if they abandoned writing? All these and many more questions would obviously concern not only writing itself but also the reading of what is written.

These are simple questions only at first glance. A comprehensive book would be required just to grasp them all. But the crux of the matter is that such a book would be a book. Instead of what? That is the question.

Superscript

My intention in this book is to write about writing. It is, if you think about it, a project turned in on itself. It makes writing both the object (that one is facing) and the instrument one uses to deal with the object. Such an undertaking cannot be compared with thinking something over, in which ideas are directed against ideas. But this comparison shows how reflection is different from an attempt to write about writing. The particle *over* in the construct *to think something over* can be interpreted in two ways: on one hand, as the effort to let supplementary ideas follow after those that have already been thought to put them in order, and on the other hand, as the effort to let ideas run counter to those already thought to track them down. Neither strategy makes any sense when writing about writing. It can't be about putting the writing one is writing about in order because it is already in order. Written signs are arranged in lines, and each one already has a designated place in this one-dimensional order. And it can't be about tracking down writing, for written signs consist of nothing but tracks (Greek: *topoi*). Writing about writing is itself to be seen as thinking of a sort, that is, as an attempt to arrange those ideas that have already been thought about writing in an order, to track down these thoughts that have been thought and to write them down. That is the intention here.

Thinking and writing about writing should really be called *superscript.*[1] Regrettably, that word is already in use and means something else. But it doesn't matter: with permission, the word *superscript* will be used with the new meaning suggested. Aren't there people who would call such violence against language "creative"?

All writing is "right": it is a gesture of setting up and ordering written signs. And written signs are, directly or indirectly, signs for ideas. So writing is a gesture that aligns and arranges ideas. Anyone who writes must first have thought. And written signs are the quotation marks of right thinking. On first encounter, a hidden motive appears behind writing: one writes to set one's ideas on the right path. That is really the first impression one has in looking at written texts: exactly this order, this alignment. All writing is orderly, and that leads directly to the contemporary crisis in writing. For there is something mechanical about the ordering, the rows, and machines do this better than people do. One can leave writing, this ordering of signs, to machines. I do not mean the sort of machines we already know, for they still require a human being who, by pressing keys arranged on a keyboard, orders textual signs into lines according to rules. I mean grammar machines, artificial intelligences that take care of this order on their own. Such machines fundamentally perform not only a grammatical but also a thinking function, and as we consider the future of writing and of thinking as such, this might well give us pause for thought.

Writing is about setting ideas in lines, for unwritten ideas, left to their own devices, run in circles. This circling of ideas, where any idea can turn back to the previous one, is called *mythical thinking* in certain contexts. Written signs are quotation marks signaling the onset of linear, directional thinking within mythical thinking. This directional thinking is called *logical thinking* for reasons still to be discussed. Written signs are quotation marks for logical thinking. This becomes clear if one looks more closely at quotation marks, that is, inverted commas. For example, 'word' is a word, but 'sentence' is not a sentence. Such a thing can only be written, for anyone who were to try to say it would be thinking in circles. In a broader, very important sense, all written signs are quotation marks.

But lines of writing not only direct ideas into rows, they direct those ideas toward a recipient. They run past their end point toward a reader. Writing is motivated by an impulse not only to direct ideas but also to direct them toward another. Only when a piece of writing reaches another, a reader, does it achieve this underlying intention. Writing is not only a reflective, inwardly directed gesture but is also an expressive, outwardly directed (political) gesture. One who writes presses into his own interior and at the same time outward toward someone else. These contradictory pressures lend writing the tension that has made it capable of carrying and transmitting Western culture and of endowing this culture with such an explosive form.

In this first observation of writing, it is the rows, the linear flow of written signs, that make the strongest impression. They make writing seem to express a one-dimensional thinking and so, too, a one-dimensional feeling—desire, judgment, and conduct—a consciousness that was able, through writing, to emerge from the dizzying circles of preliterate consciousness. We know this writing consciousness because it is our own, and we have thought and read about it.

The present book is not the first "superscript." A great deal has been written about writing, if under other titles. In these titles, writing consciousness has been given various names. It has been called "critical" or "progressive," "numerate" or "narrative." But there is a common denominator among all these names. Writing consciousness should be referred to as *historical consciousness.*

The matter is more radical than it seems, for it is not as if there were a historical consciousness capable of expressing itself in various codes, writing being one of them; rather writing, this linear alignment of signs, made historical consciousness possible in the first place. Only one who writes lines can think logically, calculate, criticize, pursue knowledge, philosophize—and conduct himself appropriately. Before that, one turned in circles. And the longer one writes lines, the more historically one can think and act. The gesture of writing produces historical consciousness, which becomes stronger and penetrates more deeply with more writing, in turn making writing steadily stronger and denser. This feedback between those who write and historical consciousness lends that consciousness a rising tension that enables it to keep pushing forward. That is the dynamic of history.

It is therefore an error to suppose that there has always been history because things have always happened, to suppose that writing only recorded what had happened, to regard historical time as that period in history when people recorded events in writing. It is an error because before writing was invented, nothing happened; rather things merely occurred. For something to happen, it has to be noticed and conceived as an event (process) by some consciousness. In prehistory (the term is accurate) nothing could happen because there was no consciousness capable of conceiving events. Everything seemed to move in endless circles. Only with the invention of writing, with the rise of historical consciousness, did events become possible. When we speak of prehistoric events, we are writing supplementary history and committing anachronisms. Even more so when we speak of natural history, for then we are committing historicism. History is a function of writing and the consciousness that expresses itself in writing.

Writing, this ordering of written signs into rows, can be mechanized and automated. Machines write faster than human beings. And not only that: they can vary the rules for assembling signs (the rules of orthography) automatically. We can already see both the speed and the variability of writing in the new orthographic writing machines, word processors, however primitive they still are for now. And artificial intelligences will surely become more intelligent in the future. They will possess a historical consciousness far superior to ours. They will make better, faster, and more varied history than we ever did. History will become unimaginably more dynamic: more will happen; events will overtake one another and become more diverse. As far as we are concerned, all history can be confidently left to automated machines. Because all these mechanical and automated things make better history than we do, we can concentrate on something else. On what? That is what the present essay means when it asks, does writing have a future?

This first chapter is called "Superscript" because it is the first and announces an intention to write about writing. For reasons of symmetry, the last chapter is called "Subscript." This symmetry is in keeping with the intention of the work. It looks like an announcement that writing has been surpassed by more effective codes and that historical consciousness has been surpassed by something new that is still beyond our conceptual powers. But the chapter title "Superscript" is not meant in this way. On the contrary, the intention is that only he who has previously subscribed to everything that is hidden in writing—who is engaged in and who will eventually underwrite everything that will be lost with the loss of writing—only he has the right to write about writing. Only such a person has the right not only to write about writing but also to write past that into writing no more.

Inscriptions

Before asking whether writing could be abandoned, one must ask how writing began. Etymology may be helpful here. *Writing* comes from the Latin *scribere,* meaning "to scratch." And the Greek *graphein* means "to dig." Accordingly, writing was originally a gesture of digging into an object with something, so making use of a wedge-shaped tool (a stylus). It is true that writing is no longer done this way. Now, writing usually involves putting pigment on a surface. We write on-scriptions rather than in-scriptions—and we usually write styluslessly.

If we call on archaeology rather than etymology, it becomes uncertain whether inscription actually preceded writing on a surface. Perhaps, for example, Egyptians were the first to use pigment. We do have a myth, however, in fact one of the foundational myths of the West, that establishes the etymological precedence of engraving over painting.

According to this myth, God made his own image in clay (Hebrew: *adamah*), infused the clay with his own breath, and so created a human being (Hebrew: *adam*). Like every myth, this one is meaningful, and its content can be interpreted. For example, clay is the material (the Great Mother) in which God (the Great Father) buried his breath (spirit), and so we arose from this intercourse as material imbued with spirit. Without rejecting this interpretation, the invention of writing can be recognized in this myth. The Mesopotamian clay in the myth is shaped into a tablet, which is engraved with the holy wedge-shaped stylus, and so the first inscription (human being) was created. Of course, the two interpretations may be combined with others, leading to unsupportable (in part, esoteric) interpretations. But that is not the intention here. Here the myth is taken seriously as a depiction of the digging gesture. What did God actually do when he buried his breath in the clay?

First, he took an object in his hand (he grasped it), then he reshaped it into a parallelepiped (he worked it), and finally, he informed it (he dug forms into it). We do know that the matter did not end there: he went on to burn the informed tablets to harden them. That is not in the myth under consideration here but rather in the one that tells of the expulsion from paradise.

The preparatory grasping and working can be bracketed out of what follows, for this is about the gesture of writing. What is of interest here is the informing and the burning. Informing is a negative gesture, directed against the object. It digs holes into objects. It digs holes of "spirit" into things too full of themselves so that these things no longer condition the subject. It is the gesture of wanting-to-be-free from the stolid resistance objects present to subjects. The digging aspect of writing is an informative gesture that seeks to break out of the prison of the conditional, that is, to dig escape tunnels into the imprisoning walls of the objective world.

Although *to inform* originally meant "to dig forms into something," it has taken on a whole series of additional meanings in the present (and, in this way, it has become a term that people use to torment one another). Still, all these meanings have a common denominator: "the more improbable, the more informative."

Information is the mirror image of entropy, the reverse of the tendency of all objects (the objective world as a whole) to decay into more and more probable situations and finally into a formless, extremely probable situation. However, this tendency toward entropy, inherent in all objects, may turn on itself and accidentally lead to improbable situations (in nature, such information as spiral nebulae or human brains appear again and again). The gesture of informing characteristically expresses the intention of a subject to negate the objective tendency toward entropy. One informs (produces improbable situations) to set spirit against material that tends, absurdly, toward heat death. Writing, like digging, presses this spirit into the object to inspire it, that is, to make it improbable.

But objects are malicious. Their tendency toward entropy will eventually cause all information engraved in objects to disappear. Everything that spirit presses into objects will be forgotten in time. The absurd objective world is stronger than the subject's will to inform it. Spirit can only hope that it will take a long time before its information disintegrates. One who writes by digging can only hope that the object one has engraved doesn't decay too quickly (even if the digging writer was God). By grasping and working objects, the writer realizes that the reverse of the tendency to decay is his resistance to the spirit that wants to inform him: the better a memory is, the more laborious it is to dig into it (e.g., bronze or marble); the easier it is to dig into it (e.g., clay), the more quickly the information dug into it will disappear. Either writing remains legible for a long time, in which case, the writing is a laborious undertaking, or the writing is effortless, in which case, it will quickly become illegible. Engraving—or any sort of in-forming prior to the electromagnetic transmission of information, faces this unpleasant choice.

There is a way out of this dilemma: one can write on clay tablets and burn these tablets later. One chooses a soft object, informs it, then hardens it, to insist that it not forgotten too quickly. In this way, it is possible both to inform without appreciable objective resistance and to overcome the malice of objects for a long time. Heating tablets for the purpose of hardening their memory is a supreme achievement of the spirit, and the entire history of the West can be seen as a series of variations on this theme: from the copying of manuscripts to print to automated memories and artificial intelligences. It is about variations on one theme: produce information, pass it on, and store it safely (if possible, aere perennius) to set the free spirit of the subject, its desire to be immortal, against the malicious laziness of objects, their tendency toward heat death. Seen in this way, writing as digging, inscription, is an expression of free will.

There is another aspect of the myth of the creation of mankind, read as a model of writing as digging. It offers an insight into the critical thing about inscription (and writing as such). God forms his likeness on clay to bury his breath in this likeness. God inscribed not amorphous clay but an image. He wrote not against the given (the datum "clay") but against something made (the image "God")—against a fact, that is. The gesture of writing does not move directly against an object but rather indirectly, through an image or with the intervention of an image. He digs into clay to tear an image apart. Inscription (writing, as such) is iconoclastic.

Let etymology bear witness once again. The English *to write* (that in fact means "scratch," as does the Latin "scribere") reminds us that *scratching* and *tearing* come from the same stem. The scratching stylus is an incisor, and one who writes inscriptions is an incising tiger: he tears images to pieces. Inscriptions are the torn pieces, the cadavers of images; they are images that fell victim to the murderous incisor teeth of writing—hence the shock with which inscription was greeted by those who first received it. The ancient Jews fell on their knees in terror before the two tablets, and in the *Metamorphoses,* the Golden Age was one in which there were not yet any inscriptions: *nec verba minantia fixo aere legebantur* ("At that time there were no threatening words to be read, fixed in bronze").

The writing incisor turns against the images we have made of and from the objective world. It turns against that zone of the imaginary, magical, and ritual that we set in front of the objective world. It tears our representations of the world apart to order the parts so torn into directional lines, into countable, accountable, criticisable concepts. The myth of human creation shows the anti-magical engagement of all writing. This is why all writing is basically shocking: it shocks us out of our prescriptive notions. It tears us away from images that meant the world, and ourselves in it, to our consciousness as it was before writing.

The claim was made in a previous argument that writing seeks a way out of dizzying circular thinking and into a thinking arranged in lines. Now this can become: out of the magic circles of prehistoric thinking and into linear, historical thinking. Writing really is a transcoding of thought, a translation from the two-dimensional surface of images into a one-dimensional linear code: out of compact, blurred pictorial codes into clear, distinct written codes; out of the imaginary into the conceptual; out of scenes into processes; out of contexts into texts. Writing is a method of tearing imaginary things apart and making them clear. The further writing advances, the more deeply the writing incisor penetrates into the abysses of imaginary things stored in our memory, tearing them apart, to "describe," to "explain," to recode them into concepts. This advance of writing along lines toward the abysses of memories (of the unconscious) and toward an objective world, stripped of imaginary things, is what we call "history." It is progressive understanding.

According to the myth, God tore his likeness apart (no matter whether we take this likeness to be an anthropomorphic doll or a tablet) and, in so doing, wrote us. So he sent us into the world as his inscriptions, drove us out of paradise into the world, then burned and hardened us so that we would describe, explain, grasp, and rule the world (and ourselves). We were made in this way, written for this purpose, sent on this mission—that is our destiny. The Arabic word *maktub* means both "destiny" and "inscription." What will we give up when we replace written codes with other, more efficient ones? Surely all those anthropologies rooted directly or indirectly in the myth under discussion here. This is probably all the anthropologies we, as occidentals, have at our disposal.

The inscriptions under consideration here, this engraving of information into objects, has not been modern for a long time. Today we are surrounded not by fired clay tiles or chiseled tablets. Instead we swim in a flood of printed material, pages of paper marked with color. Not inscriptions but rather notations are the writings in which we bathe. The question to ask is this: How is notation different from inscription, and what do we do when we write something down?

Notation

Whether written signs are engraved into objects or carried on the surfaces of objects is solely a question of technology. There is a complex feedback loop between technology and the people who use it. A changing consciousness calls for a changing technology, and a changing technology changes consciousness. Producing tools out of bronze rather than stone both expressed a changing consciousness and opened on to a new form of consciousness. One can justly speak of a Stone Age people and a Bronze Age people—or of a people that write in material and a people that write on it.

The most striking technical difference between the two writing methods is this: a stylus is used for inscription, a brush (or one of the brush's successors) for writing things down. The stylus is a wedge whose exact mechanical properties were recognized by the ancient Greeks at the very latest. It took physics and chemistry to see the complex behavior of a drop of pigment in a brush. The stylus is a more primitive tool than the brush. On the other hand, brushing is more comfortable than chiseling. A stylus is structurally simpler and functionally more complex than a brush. That is the mark of progress: everything becomes structurally more complex to become functionally simpler. (More evidence that writing-in came before writing-down.)

People brushed rather than chiseled to be able to write faster and more easily. The speed of writing is the basic difference between writing-in and writing-down. One picks up a brush or quill (a natural brush) to write as if feathered, winged, as if in flight. Then one turns the quill around and writes with the tip to write still faster. (Incidentally, this turning of the quill, this anti-Oriental, Western gesture, deserves closer consideration.) After the goose quill came faster and faster writing instruments: ballpoint pen, typewriter, and word processor—faster and faster quills. Western writers are feathered creatures.

Inscriptions are laborious, slow, and therefore considered writings. They are *monuments* (*monere*, "to consider"). Notes are writings thrown in passing onto surfaces with the intention of instructing a reader by means of a message. They are *documents* (*docere*, "to teach"). Inscriptions are monumental; notations are documentary. This difference is not always clear. As the Romans were scratching into the wax tablets with their gravers, their concern was to hold on to the things they had grasped. They wanted to document. And as monks with their goose quills laid one holy letter after another onto the parchment, laboriously and with consideration, their concern was to contemplate godliness—to erect monuments to it. It's hard to shake the feeling that the Romans would have been better off with brushes and the monks with chisels.

Our literature is not monumental (as, say, Mesopotamian literature is). It does not demand consideration and contemplation. It is documentary, it teaches and instructs. Our literature wants doctors rather than wise men. It is written quickly to be read quickly. And this speed explains the dynamics of the ever-increasing flow of literature in which we are swimming.

Quills and their successors are channels. Whether they are tubes, they usually carry black ink to be laid on a surface that is usually white. The writing hand, holding the pen, directs the channel to lay ink down in the form of written signs. So the writer is a designer rather than a painter. He does not put ink on the surface to cover it up so that the ink could put something forward; rather he produces a contrast between the color of the ink and that of the surface so that the signs become clear and distinct (black and white). The intention is not to be imaginative but rather to be unambiguous (legible in one way only). Writing does not express magical and condensed thought but rather discursive, historical thought.

A writer is one who places signs, a draftsman, a designer, a semi-ologist. And he is in fact a very fast draftsman. His drawing is called *sketching,* a word that comes from the Greek root *sche,* meaning "seize." Unlike inscriptions, notational writings are sketches and are schematic. They convey a sense of haste and an absence of leisure, of winged writing and reading. Any literary criticism should really start from this, the hectic character of what is under consideration. Criticism does not usually do this because, as a rule, it is not obvious from the texts themselves that they were thrown together in haste. On the contrary, one finds many places in them—just because it is impossible to write in one sitting—where interruptions and pauses appear to invite reflection. It is important to take these unavoidable gaps (epochs) in writing into account.

Quills must be removed again and again to dip them into the inkwell. Even a typewriter, technically relatively advanced, must have its ribbon changed from time to time. No stream of ink, how-ever advanced, is exempt. Even the surfaces to be covered are not without limits, for a new page must be inserted when the first one is full. Only when notation is replaced with teletype does it become technically possible to write in an uninterrupted stream.

Even should such tangible, objective brakes on notation be overcome, however, a continuous flow of writing would not be possible. Orthographic rules (whether logical or syntactic, or in the case of the alphabet, phonetic and musical) are calculations; that is, they require intervals between the signs. These intervals must be inserted between words, sentences, paragraphs, and chapters. The gesture of notation is staccato because the code of writing itself is particulate (discrete).

That the gesture of writing is at once hectic and intermittent refers back to the consciousness of one who writes, the conscious-ness structured as historical. We do write (and think) hastily and schematically (the full stop, rushing toward the future), but we write asthmatically. We always have to stop to catch our breath.

This inner dialectic of writing and its associated consciousness, this thinking that is driven by a pressing impulse, on one hand, and forced into contemplative pauses, on the other, is what we call "critical thinking." We are repeatedly forced to come up from the flow of notation to get a critical overview. Notation is a critical gesture, leading to constant interruptions. Such crises demand criteria. What is true of notation is true for all history.

The simultaneously hectic and stuttering, schematic and critical character of notation offers deep insight into a structure of thinking (and behavior) that is set up in lines, that is, into a structure of thinking occurring in time that rushes from the past toward the future, passing through the present without stopping. Such time is existentially untenable. For the present we rush past is exactly the place where we are "there": the present is wherever we are. It is therefore the site where the world—in fact, the past as well as the future—is realized (is made present). The future is the horizon of the present, from which the possibilities come and to which we in the present look to realize these possibilities, to make them present. The past is nothing (it's over), unless it is lifted into the present. Thought (and behavior) that rushes through the present without stopping is existentially false thought (and behavior).

As long as people wrote inscriptions, slowly, with effort and consideration, the madness of historically structured thought remained hidden. This good old time passed slowly and peacefully, not yet being really Heraclitean. Such time was livable. But with notation, progress began to accelerate. Now it is racing. Historical consciousness only really got going with notation. It is intolerable, this abandonment of everything real in favor of mere possibilities, all being in favor of becoming. That is the underlying reason we are continually forced to interrupt our writing, that we can't avoid landing in a crisis. Progress carries us along with it, but we continually bob up above it so as not to completely lose contact with reality, so as not to become completely progressive, mad.

It is beginning to become clear that continuous notation, continuous and accelerating progress, concerns apparatuses. It is enough to observe the breathless speed with which videotexts appear on terminals, for example. Apparatuses have no existential brakes: they don't exist, and they don't need to come up for air. And so we can leave progress, historical thinking and action, to apparatuses. They do it better. And we can free ourselves from all history, become mere observers of it, and become open to something else—to a concrete experience of the present.

Writings are not suitable codes for such observation or spectatorship. Images are more appropriate. We are just about to leave notation (writing as such) to apparatuses and focus our attention on making and looking at images. We are about to emigrate into the "universe of technical images" so that we can look down from there at history being written by apparatuses. But this colonization is an extremely complex process. Writing cannot just be overcome. For one thing, the images we contemplate feed on history (the apparatuses); for another, these images program history (the apparatuses); for a third, these apparatuses do not write in the same way we did; rather they use other codes. History written (and made) by apparatuses is another history. It is no longer history in the literal sense of the word. Emigration into the universe of technical images is a complex process primarily because it stumbles on literal thinking, on letters.

Notation is first and foremost literary, literal writing, whether other kinds of signs, such as Arabic numerals, appear in it. The laborious emigration to a postliterate universe of technical images demands that we reflect on letters before we repudiate them and consign them to the past.

Letters of the Alphabet

The alphanumeric code we have adopted for linear notation over the centuries is a mixture of various kinds of signs: letters (signs for sounds), numbers (signs for quantities), and an inexact number of signs for the rules of the writing game (e.g., stops, brackets, and quotation marks). Each of these types of signs demands that the writer think in the way that uniquely corresponds to it. Writing equations requires a different kind of thinking from writing rules of logic or the words of language. We are unaware of the mental leaps we are obliged to make when we read and write only because we meekly follow the apparently smooth lines. In the present essay, we are concerned with the mode of thought that corresponds to the characters characteristic of alphanumeric code. Works of writing are called, after all, "literature" (meaning quantities of letters), and we speak of a "literary" (literal) heritage.

Excursus: Numbers

A typewriter is built to arrange signs into lines. The resulting order is suited to letters but not to numbers—evidence that in alphanumeric code, letters have overpowered numbers. It is actually possible, with certain special moves, to make a typewriter reproduce mathematical equations or complicated formulas from physics, but it is easy to see that these signs form lines only with effort, by force. The assault on numbers by letters concerns a violation of numerical by literal thought. It concerns, that is, an important feature of thought supported by alphanumeric code, which is to say Western thought.

Because letters are signs for spoken sounds, an alphabetic text is a score for an audible performance: it makes sounds visible. Numbers, on the other hand, are signs for ideas, for images seen with an inner eye (2 as a sign for the mental picture of a pair). Numbers can, of course, designate exceptionally abstract images so that only a practiced eye is able to draw out the intended image. So letters codify acoustic perceptions, whereas numbers codify optical perceptions. Letters belong to the field of music, numbers to that of the visual arts. Neurophysiology, in fact, suggests that letters and numbers mobilize different brain functions and that both halves of the brain behave differently depending on whether numbers or letters are being read. Alphanumeric code appears to produce a dislocation in the brain that causes letters to suppress numbers.

The dialectic between word and image (*logos* and *eidos*) does not appear only in the inner tension of alphanumeric code. It is especially clear in alphanumerically coded texts. In a page of scientific text, for example, one sees lines of letters interspersed with islands of numbers. The eye follows the lines from left to right and stops at the islands, where it circles. The lines of letters demand that the message be translated into something audible somewhere in the brain. The eye itself, on the other hand, can see what is meant by the number islands (the algorithms). It need only follow the threads connecting the separate elements of the algorithm. So reading letters is one-dimensional, whereas reading numbers is a two-dimensional movement. Letters are about a discourse, numbers about content. A page of scientific text therefore has the same structure as a page of a picture book. The lines of letters describe the algorithms (the pictures), and these illustrate the lines of letters. The islands of numbers in scientific text should be regarded as exceptionally abstract images subordinated to a discourse.

But that is not the view represented by contemporary art criticism. Art critics do not recognize scientific algorithms as works of art—they are probably not experienced enough to recognize the power of visualization these constructs represent. Contemporary art criticism is not only blind with respect to scientific equations, it is also deaf with respect to linear scientific texts. So we're not used to recognizing a Bach fugue flowing around and flooding over Mondrian forms in a scientific text. We are not used to applying any aesthetic criteria to scientific texts, although such a criticism of science would be productive in terms of perception theory. It might proceed something like this.

A scientific text differs from a Bach fugue and a Mondrian image primarily in that it raises the expectation of meaning something "out there," for example, atomic particles. It seeks to be "true," adequate to what is out there. And here aesthetic perception is faced with a potentially perplexing question: what in the text is actually adequate to what is out there? Letters or numbers? The auditory or the visual? Is it the literal thinking that describes things or the pictorial that counts things? Are there things that want to be described and others that want to be counted? And are there things that can be neither described nor counted—and for which science is therefore not adequate? Or are letters and numbers something like nets that we throw out to fish for things, leaving all indescribable and un-countable things to disappear? Or even, do the letter and number nets themselves actually form describable and countable things out of a formless mass? This last question suggests that science is not fundamentally so different from art. Letters and numbers function as chisels do in sculpture, and external reality is like the block of marble from which science carves an image of the world.

To criticize scientific texts using such an aesthetics of percep-tion is, however, far less comfortable than it first appears. It would even be straightforward if it were possible to refer the rules of letters (logic) to the rules of numbers (mathesis). For then one could say that the letters and numbers (the auditory and visual forms of perception) have the same basic structure and that this basic structure is somehow appropriate to things out there. But a complete reduction of logic to mathematics has, unfortunately, proven impossible. Gödel has shown why it is impossible even to try. We must accept that we are condemned, on the basis of our perceptual organs and our central nervous systems, to live in at least two realities that cannot be unified: in the auditory, one of letters, and in the visual, one of numbers. It becomes clear that scientific texts try to bridge this fundamental disjunction between ear and eye by subordinating the eye to the ear. It is an extremely unpleasant epistemological proposition.

In the meantime, numbers are beginning to free themselves from letters. We are witnessing a revolution to give the eye precedence over the ear. So far the ear still dominates, and music is our best way of justifying everything else we have set in motion.

The instrument that best characterizes the contemporary upheaval is a counting device. The computer appears to be slowly (and inexorably) taking over one human intellectual function after another: calculation, logical thinking, decision making, forecasting. Under the influence of this counting device, science is drawing a picture of the world that is composed of countable pebbles (calculi), like a mosaic, and not only at the level of inanimate nature (atomic particles) but also at the level of the animate (gene). Even society is seen as a mosaic, within which the building blocks (individuals) link and detach themselves according to calculable rules. Our own thinking is understood to be a calculating of quantifiable elements. What was once regarded as a process, wavelike, linear, is now dissected into particles and computed on to curves that can then be projected in any direction (e.g., into the future). Faced with a problem, be it physical, biological, social, or psychological, we no longer try to describe it; rather we make a diagram of it. We don't think literally anymore, but numerically, no longer with the ear but rather with the eye. Our continuing use of names rather than numbers should be considered a passing stage.

It isn't true that we're in the realm of numbers, however. The world of numbers that is moving into the foreground is no longer the one whose divinity was celebrated by the Pythagoreans. It is far more primitive and methodical. As they migrate from alphanumeric into digital codes, numbers behave differently. They no longer form islands of algorithms rich in complex and creative visionary power; they form heaps that can be picked at. Even something as simple as the decimal system that ordered numbers has been abandoned in favor of the infantile binary system. The world of numbers has become more primitive because it is artificial, rather than human intelligences that are doing the counting. These intelligences are stupider but far faster. They are not capable of carrying out the elegant mathematical operations we have developed over centuries, but they don't need to, either. For all of these operations were intended to reduce the time needed to methodically add up many numbers. Artificial intelligences add with a speed that approaches that of light.

That computation has been forcibly reduced to its most primitive level is crucial to an understanding of the present revolution. Computation, the manipulation of numbers in general, can be mechanized—and it is beneath human dignity to be concerned with matters that can be left to machines. The New Man stands above numbers, not under them. He sits in front of a computer and commands it. He no longer idolizes numbers but rather plays with them, and they obey him. This attitude toward numbers is not entirely new—there have always been glass bead games like the abacus and dice. On the other hand, the game strategies that are becoming available to us are breathtakingly new. With mechanically manipulated numbers, we can play in a way that transforms numbers into the support and springboard for a completely new visionary capacity. For the moment, we are still clumsy. But a few examples can suggest the possibilities concealed within such number games.

We can order the computer to light up cone shapes in various colors on the screen, then to have them turn, collide, entangle themselves with one another, even to vibrate acoustically, like strings; that is, we can order it to make the concept of a "cone" experiential. Or we can order the computer to separate body surfaces into particles and to play with these particles (this wire netting) so as to make bodies appear on the screen that would once have been considered impossible. In short, we can order it to make real what was once impossible—to act creatively. Or we can order the computer to visualize equations that are opaque and that therefore cannot be represented (e.g., fractals) on the screen. That is to say, we can order it to make something completely abstract into something concrete so that it can be experienced, thereby expanding our experience in adventurous ways.

Now that numbers are beginning to liberate themselves from the pressure of letters and computing is being mechanized, their visionary power can unfold. Having undergone centuries of purification through the discipline of clarity and distinctness, numbers can now serve creative vision as they have never and nowhere been able to do before. Our experiences, observations, values, and actions will be enlarged immeasurably in this way. Several things obstruct this utopian view of a free, exact, clear, and distinct creative eye, however. The first of these is certainly our own conceptual categories that keep us from risking a plunge into adventure.

We speak of "computer art" when we are looking at the new images on monitors, as if we were concerned only with a new technique for producing images. By using the category "art," we block our own access to these images. Computer keys simulate mental processes. These glowing images are nearly unmediated—if *unmediated* means anything to such estranged creatures as human beings—images drawn from the brain outward. It is therefore misleading to call these published and particularized dreams "art" without adding that all previous art is only a hesitant approach to these images. Even understood in this way, however, the concept of art is a category that bypasses these images. Most computer images produced so far have been fabricated in laboratories, not in artists' ateliers transfigured by Benjamin's aura. Images produced in laboratories make at least as strong an aesthetic impact as those produced by so-called computer artists. Such images disregard the boundary between the category "art" and the category "science and technology." Science presents itself as an art form and art as a source of scientific knowledge.

This does not address the crucial feature of the inadequate categories we have inherited. For if the eye (in the form of numbers) is beginning to predominate over the ear (in the form of letters), then it will be theoretically as well as practically possible to manipulate (digitalize) auditory perception numerically. So-called computer music is only one embryonic example of it. Numbers will soon make sounds visible and images audible. "Electronic intermix" is just one first step in this direction. For some time, in fact, is has been possible to anticipate the collapse of the boundary between music and the visual arts and even the rise of mathematics. *Composition* is a synonym for *computation,* and even for Pythagoras, the lyre lay close to the triangle.

This utopia that is appearing to our unbelieving eyes and our eye-compliant ears, this utopia where numbers migrate from Platonic heaven into artificial intelligences to serve our powers of visualization, is not new but rather ancient, at least as old as the Greeks. At highly inspired moments, they spoke of *musike kai mathematike techne* as the means of attaining wisdom. This utopia, this method, this technology is now attainable—which is not to say that we will attain it. It is possible to count any process in particles, to compute it into a curve, then to project the curve into the future (to futurize it), and even, should one feel like it, to make it vibrate acoustically. But there are also random events that will, with a probability bordering on certainty, keep the curves from behaving as we project them. The preceding reflections should be read with such reservations in mind.

Letters belong to the oldest culturemes we have. In the fifteen hundred years since their invention, their original form has changed repeatedly, and yet it remains recognizable: the two horns of the Semitic steer (Hebrew: *aleph*) in the *A,* the two domes of the

Semitic house (Hebrew: *beth*) in the *B,* the hump of the Semitic camel (Hebrew: *gimul*) in the *C.* Letters are pictures of a cultural scene as it was perceived by those who invented the alphabet in the second millennium B.C. on the eastern Mediterranean. They are pictograms of things like steers, houses, and camels. And because the letters are so ancient, the archaizing word *Buchstaben* is used for them in German rather than *Buchenstäbe,*[1] although they come from a Semitic area and not from a German *Buchenwald* (beech forest).

We no longer use letters as pictograms for ancient things but rather as signs for roughly the first sound of the Semitic words that name these things. But why do we make spoken sound visible when we write? Why, when we want to get an idea down on paper, do we take this convoluted detour through the spoken language instead of using signs for ideas, that is, ideograms, as Chinese or some new computer codes do? Is it not much easier to write "2" than "two"? There must have been weighty reasons that led the Sumerian inventors of the alphabet to such a counterintuitive code as the one they inserted between thinking and writing. It is possible to investigate the reason.

Letters' obscure development from pictograms through rebuses is not at issue here; rather the question is concerned with cause: what motivated people to write alphabetically and through a spoken language? That is not a historical question but rather an absolutely contemporary one. In it lies an awareness of the decision we are facing: to give up the alphabet in favor of a code that is no longer spoken.

The alphabet is a clear rejection of ideographic writing. Despite all the ideogram's advantages, writing was to be in letters.

Ideograms are signs for ideas, for images seen with the inner eye. The preservation of images, however, was exactly what writing sought to avoid. Writing set out to explain images, to explain them away. Pictorial, fanciful, imaginative thinking was to yield to conceptual, discursive, critical thinking. It was necessary to write alphabetically rather than ideographically to be able to think iconoclastically. This is the reason for denoting the sounds of a language.

In speech, one talks "about" ideas and "about" images and, in doing so, stands above imagistic thinking, speaking down from on high. As the score of a spoken language, the alphabet permits us to stabilize and discipline a transcendence of images that has been won, with effort, through speech. One writes alphabetically to maintain and extend a level of consciousness that is conceptual, superior to images, rather than continually falling back into pictorial thinking, as we did before writing was invented.

We know that the alphabet has proven to be a remarkably productive invention. It has facilitated discourse that was never achieved in nonalphabetic areas: Greek philosophy, medieval theology, the discourses of the modern sciences. Without the alphabet, there would have been no such discourses, for they are conceptual, critical discourses that detach themselves further and further from imagination, becoming more and more abstract, more unimaginable. In the process, it becomes clear that the alphabet cannot do without ideograms. The discourse of modern science is impossible without numbers. Although ideograms are signs for pictures, they can scale heights of abstraction inaccessible to language-bound thought. The question arises whether the alphabet as the code of pure conceptual thought really was a lucky break. Perhaps binding thought to language inhibited our extraordinary capacity for abstraction so that this capacity could only develop in the areas of mathematics and symbolic logic. Perhaps the surpassing of the alphabet will offer these capacities new avenues for development such as that of synthetic images. Perhaps without the alphabet, we would have been still more iconoclastic (of course, our culture would have turned out much differently). In the matter of consigning the alphabet to history, such considerations are pertinent.

To say that the alphabet was invented to write concepts rather than ideas is by no means to say it all. For how is the long detour through language to be explained? Something in the spoken language itself calls out to be fixed in place—and in fact, not so much in the memories of speakers and hearers, or in records or tapes, but rather in writing itself. Spoken language seems to rush toward writing almost on its own, to become a written language and so to achieve its full maturity. After the invention of writing, spoken language appears to be a preparation for a written language, to teach people how to speak properly in the first place.

Today we have hardly any access to preliterate speech. Even in nurseries and among illiterates, writing has permeated the language. We can reconstruct the way people spoke before the invention of writing, however, *mythically*, meaning "with mouth closed." The root word can be recognized in the Latin *mutus* (mute).

From our contemporary perspective, people then stuttered and stammered. They engaged in discourse (if by *discourse*, we mean a flow of sounds from one mouth into the ear of another). But it didn't have a direction. It wasn't a proper discourse: it ran into obstacles (refutations), went backward, turned itself in a circle, and ended in silence. Since the romantic era, we've become accustomed to seeking wisdom in these mythical utterances and, of course, to finding it. It is also possible to claim that people of that time babbled.

With the help of the alphabet, the mythical babble was leveled so that it could run along a clear line toward an exclamation, question mark, or full stop instead of turning itself in circles, so that it could begin to raise proper questions, issue proper orders, narrate, and explain things properly. The alphabet was invented to replace mythical speech with logical speech and so to be able, literally for the first time, to "think."

Children and illiterates are inducted into the code of letters, learning first spelling and not reading. They learn signs to be able to jump from them into the signified, into the spoken language. They learn to speak properly right from the start. And when they have learned it, spoken language becomes a phenomenon they approach with the help of signs. They no longer speak as it comes naturally. (They leave that to the gabblers; rather they speak literary German, Oxford English, French of the Encylopédie, or Dante's Italian. They speak properly.)

The alphabet does not write spoken language down; rather it writes it up, lifting and taking hold of it to bring it into the order of its rules. In this way, the alphabet also orders and regulates that which is meant by language: thinking. And so for those who are able to write, spoken language becomes more than a medium through which they express themselves (as it is for illiterates and children); language is rather the material against which they press the alphabet, against which they literally ex-press. In short, they work on the language. Only at the point when language ceases to be a means (a medium) and begins to be a purpose does the essence of alphabetic writing come into view.

A writer forces the spoken language to accommodate itself to orthographic rules. Language defends itself. Each language defends itself according to its character. German is slippery, English brittle, French deceptive, Portuguese sly. The writer's linguistic work is an assault on a language that twists, slides away, shatters, and seduces him as he grasps it. Writing literally has the tone of a quarrel between lovers, between the one who writes and the language *(odi et amo)*. In this lovers' quarrel, we see what language is capable of doing: its capacities exceed all expectations.

Unfortunately, literary criticism, above all romantic literary criticism, allowed itself to be carried away in the turmoil of the struggling writer. And in fact, there is something that happens in writing that cool words fail to convey. The writer presses the letters, these dead marks, against the living body of the language so that they can suck life out, and lo and behold: these vampires take on an eventful life of their own under his fingers. No wonder he swoons, feeling his life energies have been spent. Literary criticism speaks of the work of creating language.

At the distance afforded by information theory, the writing

process can be described somewhat differently, say, like this: the alphabet forces the language into the chains of its orthographic rules. In this way, language is distorted, taking on forms that would have otherwise been improbable. *Improbable* is a synonym for *informative,* making it right to say that the alphabetic writing has been continually drawing new information out of language for three and a half millennia. Since its invention, writing has been carving and chiseling every language available to us, always trying to bring new information to light. So these languages have become extremely fine and valuable instruments. No writer has ever encountered a virgin language, a language that has not already passed through the beds of countless rapists. In his struggle with language, a writer reworks the information of previous writers freshly, producing new information from it, passing it on to the next writers so that they may produce new information in turn. The process of writing is a discourse of thousands of years that has continually generated new information, with which every single writer is in dialogue. Even if this was not the inventor's intention, the invention of the alphabet has shaped discourse in these ways.

There have apparently been two results of the inquiry into the hidden impulses behind the invention of the alphabet. One suggests that the inventor was iconoclastic: writing would not indicate images (nor ideograms) but rather sounds, so that consciousness might free itself from pictorial, magical thinking. The other conclusion suggests that the inventor's intention was to construct a linear discourse: writing was to indicate sounds so that mythical, circular, halting speech could be replaced by consequential speech. On closer consideration, however, it becomes clear that these two answers say the same thing.

The inventor of the alphabet saw image making and mythmaking as enemies, and he rightly made no distinction between the two. Image making and image worship (magic), like dark, circular tales (myth), are two sides of the same coin. The motivation behind the invention of the alphabet was to supersede magical–mythical (prehistoric) thought and to make room for a new (historical) consciousness. The alphabet was developed as the code of historical consciousness. If we should give up the alphabet, it will surely be because we are trying to supersede historical consciousness. We are tired of progress, and not only tired: historical thinking has shown itself to be murderous and mad. That (and not the technical disadvantages of the alphabet) is the real reason we are prepared to abandon this code.

Texts

In their battle against the spoken language, characters of the alphabet (which are basically nothing but dead letters, invented to spin the magical promise of myth out into lines) suck the life of the language up into themselves: letters are vampires. Lines formed from these letters that have come alive are called "texts." Etymologically, the word *text* means a textile and the word *line* a linen thread. But texts are unfinished textiles: they consist of lines (the woof) and are not held in place by vertical threads (the warp) as a finished textile would be. Literature (the universe of texts) is half finished. It seeks completion. Literature is directed toward a receiver, from whom it demands completion. The writer weaves threads that are to be picked up by the receiver to be woven in. Only then does the text achieve a meaning. A text has as many meanings as it has readers.

The well-known phrase *habent [sua] fata libelli* (books have destinies) gives only a rough idea of what is meant here. It is not that the writer transmits powers to his texts so that the text can put those powers into play according to its particular dynamics; it is that the text goes out to be completed. So the text does not *have* a destiny; it *is* a destiny. In other words, the text is meaning-full, and this fullness can only be exploited (explained) by each of its readers in a particular way. The greater the number of ways a text can be read, the more meaningful it is. Artistotelian texts are meaningful because they have meant something to Alexandrian readers different from what they meant to Thomas Aquinas, Hegel, Galileo, or twentieth-century historians. A text meets its fate (the message that it is) in its receiver. Texts without receivers, unread texts, are meaningless lines of letters that take on meaning only when they are read.

Oddly, there are lapses in awareness that texts are media (bridges supported as much by the receiver's as by the sender's pylon). There are writers who forget that, by their very structure, texts are directed toward others and are meaningless in isolation. Forgetting others while writing is the result of forgetting oneself. Armed with his letters, a writer struggles against a resistant language. He wants to take hold of the language—and that which is meant by it as well, namely, his thoughts, feelings, intuitions, and desires. The struggle is absorbing, making him forget himself and everyone else. Writing is an intoxicating enterprise. In fact, those texts written un-self-consciously are among the most important we possess. It is one among countless contradictions that lie in wait for us within writing.

Let us distinguish between two types of text. One type communicates, informs, transmits. The other is expressionistic, intense, written under pressure. An example of the first type would be scientific communication, of the second, lyric poetry. These extreme examples could mislead us into dividing the whole of literature into two branches, one that consciously seeks to be read and another that is unaware of this intention. But the following consideration argues against such a literary criticism: most communicative texts want to be comfortably received, to be easy to read. They must therefore be denotative; that is, they must transmit a message with a single meaning. As a result, any reader will interpret such texts in the same way. Scientific texts, especially those that make extensive use of numerical signs, are easy to receive, even if they appear difficult to an uninitiated reader. Their difficulty lies not in the text but in the codification that must be learned beforehand. There are texts that appear to be scientific but are nevertheless dark. This is especially the case with some texts in the humanities. The literary criticism proposed here would be able to show on formal grounds that such texts were not scientific but merely presented themselves as such.

Expressionistic texts, on the other hand, pay no attention to the receiver. They can afford to be difficult to read. They can be connotative (dark), which is to say that they can transmit multiple meanings. The result is that such a text can be interpreted by each of its readers in a different way. Are expressionistic texts therefore more meaningful than communicative ones? The literary criticism proposed here would be forced to the paradoxical conclusion that the very branch of literature that is unaware of its communicative intention transmits the more meaningful messages.

But it is unnecessary to pursue such a literary classification any further. Consciously, communicative texts can be exceptionally connotative. An example is the Bible, the founding text of the West. The Bible is a text that seeks to be read by any reader whatsoever and to be interpreted by each in his own way. It speaks to all, and to each in a manner of his own choosing. It is destiny and wants to be. At the same time, the Bible is expressive, written under pressure. In this sense, it is a model for all texts, for it was written in an un-self-conscious state and in an awareness of others. This awareness of others extends to the disposition of the Hebrew "original" of the Bible to be continually translated by others. So we speak of the destiny of the Septuagint, the Vulgate, the King James, and the Luther Bible as well as the unfolding destinies of original texts, many of which have been lost. The unfolding of the destiny of the West, inasmuch as it can be seen in the history of biblical texts, could serve as a model for the structure of the history of ideas, although the Bible challenges the familiar axiom of communication theory that says that "the better one communicates, the less information he transmits, and the more information to be transmitted, the more difficult it is to communicate it."

Texts are half finished. Their signs rush toward an end point but past this toward a reader who, they hope, will complete them. It makes no difference whether the writer is aware of it, or even whether, like Kafka, he expressly rejects a completing reader; texts are a search for the Other. Of course, it is possible to divide up the universe of texts according to various criteria, but all texts are outstretched arms trying, whether optimistically or in despair, to be taken up by another. This is what the gesture of writing is disposed to do.

For whom am I there when I write? That is the political question of a society dominated by writing: in such a society, the truly political gesture is to write and publish texts. All other political engagement follows from and submits to texts. If we pose the previous question in the concrete context of the textual universe rather than in a vacuum, it becomes clear that I, the one who writes, am there not for everyone but for the audience I am able to reach. The illusion that I write for everyone is not only megalomaniacal but also a symptom of false political consciousness. A writer can reach only that audience with whom he is linked through the channels that transmit his text. He therefore writes not directly to his readers but rather to his transmitters. He is there first and foremost for his transmitters, and *first* is to be taken literally. From the first to the last line, a text is written for its transmitter. The entire text is imbued with its primary commitment to its transmitters. No literary criticism should disregard this fact. The transmitter stands not outside but in the center of any text. Since the invention of the book press, the transmitter has usually been the publisher.

A publisher is a grid in the stream of texts whose duty is to block most texts from getting into print. The vast swell of printed texts in which we currently swim is just the tip of an iceberg of texts that did not succeed in passing through the grid.

A text is an expression with the conscious or unconscious intention of making an impression. Texts that remain unprinted are expressions that made a poor impression on the publisher. They did not pass through the publisher's criteria (the holes in the grid) and so save their lives. "To make a bad impression" means not to have met the criteria of the one to be impressed. This poses the question of criteria of censorship (the way the grid is constructed).

Although we can see the beginnings of automated censorship everywhere (e.g., in the editorial policy of the mass media), publishers have not so far become automata. At the moment, publishers are still sufficiently elastic to adjust themselves to suit some of the texts seeking to meet their criteria. There are still dialogues between publishers and texts that can change the publisher's criteria. (The degree of elasticity a publisher enjoys may, incidentally, serve to gauge the level of freedom available in a particular society.) This dialogue between texts and publisher may sometimes change the publishing criteria, but it also changes texts. That is, after all, the essence of dialogue: the participant becomes the other of the other, himself changing by changing another. A printed text is not only one that has changed (moved, impressed) the publisher but also one that has been changed (moved, impressed) by the publisher. The printed text is a result of a handshake between the writer and the publisher and carries the traces of both hands. Here the writer's hand has been grasped by the publisher's hand. The handshake is among the most gripping of gestures, for it is at once one of the most public and one of the most intimate: the publisher is there for the writer, the writer for the publisher, and both for the reader.

Accordingly, the pressure on the printed text, unlike that on an unprinted text, is twofold. It carries the charge of both the writer's expression and the publisher's resistance. It is a clenched fist, and as a clenched text, it is meant to impress both intentions on its future reader. It is meant—as one says unthinkingly, without being aware of the dynamics inherent in the concept—to inform a reader. To *inform* means to press a form into something that offers resistance to the pressure. With printed texts, writers and publishers have committed themselves to informing readers—to making an impression on them: first the expression of the writer, then the resistance of the publisher, then the pressure of print, and finally the impression on the readers. That is Gutenberg's dynamic of texts.

But there is still a question whether such textual dynamics are losing energy in the face of an overwhelming textual inflation, whether this loss of energy could be one of the reasons for giving up writing. The mountains of printed material that are delivered to us in our homes daily, the primeval forests in which we lose ourselves in bookstores—these are surely no longer clenched fists with which writers and publishers have sworn to inform us. They seem to be chloroformed cotton wads that publishers have produced to anesthetize us, having sought out writers suited to the purpose. Most contemporary publishing sets out to numb readers, and publisher and writer appear to be no more than functionaries in this benumbing business. They are functionaries, furthermore, who can be replaced by automatic apparatuses in the foreseeable future: publishers by programmed grids, writers by word processors, until finally the alphabet will be abandoned as an ineffective code and society will be informed (benumbed) exclusively by programmed images with sound. In other words: in the face of textual inflation and the informatic revolution, does it still make sense to write, publish, print, and read?

The question at hand concerns the clenching of fists, potentially penetrating through the anesthetizing cotton wads. It is about an aesthetic question. *Aisthetstai* means "perceive." The question is whether informative texts can be perceived at all, now and in the future, whether it is still possible for writers and publishers to conspire against an increasingly automated anesthetization industry. Such a conspiracy against numbness and in favor of information, this clenching of texts to bring them out of the Gutenberg and into the electronic era, is a strategy we know from Occam's razor. Only those texts that submit to the razor can penetrate. The more tightly the text is clenched, the more perceptible it is in the cotton wads of software.

Occam's razor goes *entia non sunt multiplicanda praeter necessitatem* (things should not be multiplied unnecessarily). It is an instrument for cutting away the unnecessary—the redundant, as it is said today. The publisher's resistance to the writer's expression is like a swipe of Occam's razor. The difference between unpublished and published texts is clear: the first go to the guillotine; the second go into battle.

Despite the carnage among texts, we're flooded with them. The publishers' guillotine has proven ineffective. Occam's razor facilitates better criteria, publishers' criteria (holes in their grids) appropriate to the transition from Gutenbergian to electromagnetic conditions. Briefly, the shorter a text—the more succinct, the better. That is an informatic criterion, implying that the less redundant a text is, the more informative it will be. The shorter it is, the truer it is as well, for everything superfluous is untrue. Einstein's equations are truer than Newton's because they rule out grams and content themselves with centimeters and seconds. The shorter a text, the better, for everything superfluous is invalid. Short instructions (laws, directions) are better than long ones because they offer behavioral models that are easier to follow.

It looks as though nothing could be simpler or therefore easier to automate than the publishing of texts. They can be shortened to an absolute minimum. Today it seems that textual criticism of any sort would have to say that only minimal texts have any prospect of surviving the informatic revolution.

Unfortunately, the matter is not so simple. There are texts that force information precisely from their redundancy (e.g., the convoluted digressions of Thomas Mann). But it is not so much for this reason as it is, above all, because there is a certain critical point at which the use of Occam's razor castrates a text rather than circumcising it. If most of the redundancies were removed, there would remain in most cases only noise and no perceptible information. The dialogical battle between the writer and the publisher is about locating this critical point, where the highest quantity of information is conveyed before the whole begins to disintegrate into noise. Finding this critical point is, finally, a publisher's determining criterion.

Texts are discourses. The written signs flow in them past an end point toward a reader who completes them. If Occam's razor slices this discourse apart, the reader will no longer be able to receive (decode) it. The shorter a text, the more difficult it is to decode. From the critical point onward, it becomes unintelligible. The battle between the writer and the publisher has to drive the difficulty of reading to its extreme point—and stay there. It has to make the highest possible demands on the reader without overwhelming him. The publisher's criterion is the reader's reading capability.

Texts must flow. Compressed letters, words, sentences, and paragraphs must follow one on the other without gaps. Particles of text must be built into a wave structure. It is about rhythm, about layered levels of rhythm. Each single level of letters, words, sentences, and paragraphs must resonate in a rhythm particular to itself, and all must resonate together. Texts must harmonize. A unified pitch must resonate on the musical, lexical, semantic, and logical levels of the text. Only if a text is in harmony can a reader agree or disagree with it, can a reader resonate in sympathy or antipathy. For this reason, Occam's razor needs not only to circumcise discourse but also to reassemble it into a harmonious unity. Publishers have to make a collage from the text, without the reader seeing it as a collage.

Texts must harmonize. There are two sorts of harmonies, rhythms. In the first, one wave of discourse follows another. In the second, they crash, foaming, into one another. This second sort of rhythm could be called "syncopation." A text is syncopated if it continually contradicts itself and still flows smoothly along. Such a text grips the reader by going against the heartbeat, tempting him into contradiction, drawing him in against his will. Such a text really is that clenched fist, striking through anesthetizing media to inform. The internal contradiction in a text, its syncopating force, is one of the consequences of the external contradiction between the writer and the publisher. True, good, and beautiful texts, that is, concise texts that flow without interruption and are nevertheless contradictory, are works of a creative dialogue between the writer and the publisher. They justify some hope that not all texts will be sacrificed to the rising universe of technical images.

The writer is above all there for his publisher, to share with him the making of a clenched fist from a half-made text. The hope is that the clenched fist will reach across informatic conditions and seize readers who will complete the text, even after alphanumeric code has become obsolete. Even if he is not always aware of his search, a writer is searching for another, a way out of his loneliness and into a community, assisted by the common ground he shares with his publisher. Before print, it was not publishers, but above all the Church, that took up the task of criticizing texts and transmitting them to readers. Writers wrote in search of the Absolute Other *(ad maiorem Dei gloriam)*. At that time, a reader transmitted the text of a writer on his way to godliness (to the completion of his text). The invention of print changed writing: a religious engagement became a political one.

Print

Typography is to be considered here less as a technology for the production of printed materials or as a method for distributing alphanumeric information than as a new way of writing and of thinking. These aspects of print are in fact of great importance for an understanding of the current information revolution (electromagnetic information can be regarded as a further development in the technology and distribution methods of print). But here we are concerned with a very radical question, namely, whether it was only with the invention of print that writers became aware of what they were actually doing by putting characters in rows, whether this theoretical and practical mastery of writing didn't exceed the historical consciousness that writing expresses, whether the information revolution can't be grasped as the result of an exhaustion of the potentiality inherent in writing.

The Greek word *typos* generally means "trace," and in this sense, such traces as those left on the beach by birds' feet could be called *typoi*. At another level, the word refers to the way these tracks can be used as models for classifying the birds that have walked by. Finally, the word means that I myself have the capacity to make such bird tracks in the sand and so to distinguish and compare various kinds of birds. So *typos* refers to that which all bird tracks have in common (the typical); it means the universal behind all that is characteristic and distinctive.

The Greek work *graphein* generally means "to dig." In this sense, such marks as those left by a stylus in clay are typographies. But we know that in ordinary language, the word *graphein* means writing.

It means the engraving of written signs, exactly these traces that classify, compare, and distinguish. So the word *typography* is really a pleonasm that could be translated as inscriptionengraving or writtensignwriting. It is entirely sufficient to say "writing."

Since writing (and particularly alphanumeric writing) was invented, people have been typographing. Gutenberg didn't really invent anything: printing would have been possible by the middle of the second millennium B.C. in this sense. All the technical requirements (presses, inks, page-shaped supports, even the art of negative casting in metal) were then already in place. But there was as yet no printing because no one was yet aware that by drawing letters, one was dealing with types. Written signs were taken to be characters. "Type-identifying" thought had not yet pressed itself into consciousness. Gutenberg's great deed was the discovery of the types inherent in alphanumeric script.

The difficulty of achieving standardizing consciousness can be illuminated through an example. The medieval dispute over universals concerned the problem of comparison. What do I do when I compare a table and a chair? Do these two objects have something in common, something to be revealed as typical? Perhaps their shared "furnitureness"? That was the view of the realists. Or must I accept that the characteristics of these two things are not comparable and that I have to pluck a word out of thin air (such as the word *furniture*) to induce a comparison where no real one is possible. That was the view of the nominalists. For the former, the typical, the universal is actually embedded in particulars and can be discovered: *universalia sunt realia.* Hence the designation "realists." For the latter, there is nothing behind particulars, and the typical is nothing but a name we invent to facilitate comparisons: *universalia sunt nomina.* Hence their designation "nominalists."

Yet this dispute is not exclusively a matter of logic (does *comparison* refer back to a common feature or is it a trick for turning unlike into like?). It really concerns an existential question; that is, if universals are real, then they must form a hierarchical pyramid. If

I can establish furnitureness in the comparison between table and chair, I must be able to proceed to a higher universal by comparing furniture with clothing, and so on to the tip of the pyramid, the universal of all universals, and from there to God. Through comparisons, then, I can approach God and save my soul, and this by two complementary methods: either through thought, by drawing broader and broader generalities out of particulars, and rising by means of this inductive method from a lower to a higher level of reality until I finally reach God by the intellectual route (philosophy and theology), or practically, through works, by extracting the general (the essence) from the particular (the accident) and from this essence to a higher one, until I finally extract the final essence of all essences (the "fifth," the *quintessence*), that is, God. From lead I can precipitate gold, from that a virgin spring, the philosopher's stone, and finally God. Through disciplined actions (e.g., alchemy), I can find God and save my soul.

If the universals are nothing but words, all philosophy and theology turns into sheer wordplay (*flatus vocis*—a breath of air produced by a voice, a vocal grunt), and all practices that seek God, such as alchemy, become the devil's work. For then I must accept that the world into which I was thrown at birth is made up entirely of unique phenomena that cannot be compared. Should I pay attention to them, my soul will become entangled, as in a trap. And so I must turn my back on this vale of tears and open myself to God in pure, inarticulate faith *(sola fide)* if I would avoid the devil and save my soul.

Whatever history books say about it, the invention of print settled the dispute over universals in favor of the realists. It is true that many nominalists have made substantial contributions to the development of modern philosophy and science, but the realist watchword *universalie sunt realia* has become a foundational idea in modern thought and research. We believe in the reality of universals, of types, in the reality of atomic particles, genes, social classes, and races, and we try to identify and manipulate them. If this belief is now beginning to wobble, if we are surreptitiously tending toward nominalism (e.g., as positivists or phenomenologists), it is because typifying thought is exhausted. It is becoming absurd.

The invention of print settled the dispute over universals in favor of the realists. Print showed clearly that when we write (and when we think in the way that is expressed in writing), we manipulate types. Print made types handy. It took them in hand. In this way, it shifted the idea of the reality of ideas (this belief that sponsored medieval realism) from the speculative into the practical. Print became one of the pillars of modern science.

Prior to Gutenberg, a writer considered written signs to be characters that made the characteristic sound of a specific spoken language visible. According to this erroneous belief, each specific language demanded a characteristic alphabet of its own, for the Latin *A* meant a different sound from the Greek alpha. There were at that time four alphabets in use simultaneously—that is, the Latin, the Greek, the Hebraic, and the Arabic—so that each language could make itself visible in its characteristic way. Now there was also a dim awareness that written signs actually were types and not characters and that it is therefore possible to refer to, say, Slavic languages with Greek letters, Germanic ones with Latin letters, and Iranian ones with Arabic letters, but this awareness remained dim: the four languages characteristic of each alphabet were held to be sacred. If these four alphabets are still preserved today, despite a clear awareness of the typology of writing, it is because remnants of the dim awareness continue to resist typifying thought today.

Print threw a clear light on the dim consciousness of types, and so, too, on the problematical (doubtful) features of this thinking. Two problems will be identified here because they illuminate the contemporary crisis in this thinking.

1. Print demonstrates that types are not unchanging, eternal forms (as Plato and the medieval realists thought) but that they can be adapted, improved, and discarded. For example, because the Latin alphabet had no sign for the German sound "sch," the type *sch* was

invented (incidentally, not an especially brilliant achievement). That did not prove the nominalist thesis that "types are pure invention." On the contrary, it meant that although there really are types, they still must be adapted to what is characteristic. The type *sch* does not hover over us in some sort of Platonic heaven, but neither can it just be plucked from the air. Rather one is forced to accommodate the sound to *sch*. In doing so, one has in fact understood the sound to be typical. The concept of "theory" is thereby changed radically. No longer does it mean a pious, passive contemplation of eternal forms, no more an empty play of words. It means a progressive modeling of better and better (and in this sense truer) types. Theories offer knowledge, but they are inventions. The seeds of this underlying problem with scientific knowledge lay in the invention of print. The contemporary crisis in historical thought is in part rooted in an awareness of this problem.

2. Something printed is a typical thing, and not a distinctive, incomparable, unique thing. A printed paper is a specimen, one among many examples of one unique thing (e.g., of a manuscript). Something printed is valuable not as a distinctive object (as this singular piece of paper) but as a type. The interesting thing about it is not the production of print (of papers, of printed writing) but the production of the types (of the text). The sight of something in print makes a mockery of the classical anthropology of *homo faber*. It confirms the Christian theory of work as punishment. In the presence of print, it becomes evident that the occupation worthy of human beings is typifying, the manipulation of signs, the "making of meaning": better, informing. Work—the production of distinctive things, comes in for distain, as a subhuman gesture to be dismissed with the flip of a switch. Among the first effects of this contempt for work and esteem for typification was the Industrial Revolution, that is, the installation of machines. Print can be understood as the model and core of the Industrial Revolution: information was to be pressed not only into books but also mechanically into textiles, metal, and plastic.

Print reaches further, past the Industrial Revolution into postindustrial society. It is the core of the current rising contempt for distinctive objects and esteem for typical, pure information. The revaluation of all standards associated with work is relevant here, and consciousness of this problem is one of the bases of the current crisis.

As writers of the Gutenberg era became aware that they were manipulating types, that they were "informaticians," they unfurled the typifying mode of thought in all areas of culture. This consists in finding types suited to distinctive features of the world, in continually improving them, and in then impressing them on the world. This way of thinking took rough form about the middle of the second millennium B.C. in the eastern Mediterranean. It pressed into consciousness clearly with print, and in modern times conquered the world. The Gutenberg galaxy reaches further back and further forward than McLuhan realized.

But there are some signs that the victory was not definitive, that is, the victory of typifying thought—this modified realism—over a previously suppressed nominalism. It is possible to hear again the nominalist objection to sweeping classification and typification of all phenomena through science, technology, politics, art, and philosophy, namely, that none of it is anything more than a "vocal grunt." Husserl's battle cry "back to the things themselves," away from typological abstraction and back to the concrete instance, is an example of this. It challenges progress. For progress—of science, technology, economics, and politics—from the concrete object to an abstract type is slowly but surely revealing itself to be destructive madness, for example, in Auschwitz, in thermonuclear armaments, in environmental pollution, in short, in the apparatuses that typify and universalize everything. We are beginning to lose faith in the reality of universals, and the nominalistic, vale-of-tears feeling has begun, with Kafka at the latest, to crystallize in and around us. Print-based thought is about to be overhauled.

The informatic revolution, this production of signs and their positioning in electromagnetic fields, openly breaks with print consciousness. The new signs that appear on computer or television screens are no longer traces engraved in objects; they are no longer "typographic." The kind of thought that is producing the new information is no longer a typographic, typifying kind of thought. The gesture of print and the mentality that expresses itself in this gesture are becoming archaic. Western, historical, typifying thought is becoming archaic. Progress is becoming archaic so that the progressive of the present will become the reactionary of the future. That said, most of us are condemned to think in a reactionary way because we have been imprinted with the trace-making mode of thought. We would prefer to go on writing and printing: we face the informatic revolution with fear and loathing.

It is fairly clear what will be lost in the transition from Gutenbergian to electromagnetic culture, namely, everything we treasure in the Western legacy. On the other hand, we do not see what we have to gain. If we could do that, we would already have reached the first step toward the new way of thinking. But by trying to immerse ourselves in nominalistic thought, say, in the life and poetry of Francis of Assisi, we can get a sense of the future. *Sola fide?*

We can regard print, this alphabetic writing that has become self-aware, as the expression of Western, historical, scientific, progressive thought. The informatic revolution makes print, the alphabet, and this kind of thought superfluous. It leads to a new mode of thought that can be anticipated but not yet perceived. That sounds like an assertion, but it is really a concerned and hopeful question directed toward the future.

Instructions

One way to anticipate the kind of thinking that characterized the informatic revolution is to observe those who manipulate the apparatus, setting the new signs into electromagnetic fields. The word *program* is the Greek equivalent of the Latin *praescriptio* and the German *Vorschrift*. Are these people continuing to write or starting again? Are contemporary reactionaries on the mark when they assert that nothing has changed fundamentally, that the essential always stays the same? To whom are these people writing? For they are not writing past a conclusion to another human being. Rather they write with and for apparatuses. Didn't the earlier discussion show that writing to other people was the essential thing about writing? So the essence of writing has changed for these people; it is another writing, in need of another name: programming. For reactionaries, this is not just uncomfortable; it is terrifying.

From a certain angle, such terror in the face of the new appears harmless. So people don't write alphabetically anymore but rather use other, so-called binary codes. Artificial intelligences are too stupid (perhaps only for the time being) to be able to decode letters. The new computer codes are in fact extraordinarily simple (as simple as artificial intelligences), but it is not simple to use them. They are structurally simple and functionally complex systems. Most of us have not mastered them; on the other hand, we have all learned the alphabet, and print has resulted in a comprehensive, democratizing literacy. The new computer codes have made us all illiterate again. A new literate caste has arisen. For most of us, the new writing (computer programs) is suffused with that kind of mystery that surrounded alphabetic writing before the invention of print. What cannot be decoded is a frightening secret. People fall to their knees *(supplex turba)* and try to appease it (the Golden Calf before the two tablets). Of course, nothing could be easier than to penetrate the mystery. One has only to learn the secret codes (in the case of the Romans and Jews, the alphabet; in our case, computer codes). But that is exactly what our fear of the new makes impossible. Learning it is child's play only for our fearless children. We have to try other things. We have to try to use a typographic way of thinking to get to grips with post-typographic "writing." Since this essay is literal, it will try to dispel a terror of programs.

If a *program* is to be understood as writing directed not toward human beings but toward apparatuses, then people have been programming since writing was invented—before there were any apparatuses. For one wrote to human beings as though they were apparatuses. One prescribed models of human behavior, and these instructions constitute a prominent thread in the advancing discursive mesh we call Western literature. Using this thread to guide us in a survey of Western history, the development can be represented as follows: at the beginning, since the Stele of Hammurabi, these instructions were called "commandments"; then, with the Twelve Tablets, they became "laws," which later branched out into decrees, regulations, and other forms of instruction; during the Industrial Revolution, instructions were added that pertained to people's behavior toward machines, or "user's manuals"; until finally, since the informatic revolutions, the program discussed earlier—namely, instructions to machines—completed this development. Programs are not only a completely new way of writing, they are also the culmination of a pattern established when writing began.

The thread of instructions just described (and with it the history of the West that is articulated in it) can be understood in various ways, for example, as a tendency toward desacralization. The commandments (say, the Ten Commandments) were holy. They had a heavenly author. It was a superhuman authority that made human beings into marionettes (apparatuses). The laws (say, constitutional law) had, if not a heavenly, at least a mythical author (e.g., the people), and this mythical authority manipulated the people's behavior. It became more and more clear subsequently that instructions were made by people manipulating other people. User's manuals revealed that all instruction seeks machine-like, automatic human behavior. This is why user's guides are shorter the more automated the machine, until, with fully automatic machines, they become superfluous. In their place are the programs. Here no human beings require instruction. Instructions can instead be issued to apparatuses. In this way, it becomes clear that the goal of instructions (and of Western history) has been completely profane behavior and that, when this goal is achieved, it is superfluous to instruct people at all or to manipulate them. They behave as they should automatically.

The thread of instructions can be read equally well as a tendency to devalue behavior, to reduce it to an object of scientific study (should "science" be understood as value-free thinking and action). The commandments prescribe behavior according to eternal values, the laws, behavior consistent with high values. Subsequent instructions tend to become value-free, until finally, user's manuals apply to functional behavior only. So it concerns a depoliticization and functionalization of behavior, which can be read from the syntactical construction of instructions. They change from imperative propositions ("thou shalt") to functional *if–then* propositions. The commandment "thou shalt honor thy father and mother" becomes advice for use: "If you want to eat chicken soup, do this and this with the tin of chicken soup." This steady devaluing of behavior concludes with programs. In logically constructed computer programs, there is no symbol for *should*. Accordingly, it becomes clear that the tendency of instructions (and of Western history as a whole) is toward a complete depoliticization of all behavior and that when this goal is achieved, human beings and their society will steer themselves automatically, like a cybernetic system.

These two readings of the tendency inherent in instructions convey some sense of the rising functional way of thinking. It is a profane, value-free thought. It can no longer be grasped in historical, political, or ethical categories. Other cybernetic, computable, functional categories must be applied to it. For this reason, programming cannot actually be called writing. It is a gesture that expresses a different kind of thought.

The question remains whether the effort undertaken earlier to demystify programming has dispelled the terror. Of course, the matter can be approached from an optimistic point of view. Because programs instruct apparatuses, the burden of instruction shifts from human beings to inanimate objects, and human beings become free to behave as they like. From this standpoint, the tendency inherent in instructions and culminating in programs is aimed at freedom. Apparatuses behave better and faster than human beings: they assemble automobiles better, they sew better, dig better, and soon will be able to do their cherry-picking more efficiently. And they think better too: they calculate, draw, and make decisions faster. (They are, curiously, better at calculation than they are at cherry-picking.) From now on, people can concentrate on programming apparatuses. Could that not be the freedom we have sought since history began?

Two quite different kinds of objections come to mind. The first one, close at hand, is fairly easy to dismiss. It is concerned that some behavior cannot be taken over by apparatuses and that the sort of behavior that cannot be automated is exactly the sort that constitutes human dignity, for example, the commandment to "honor thy father and mother." That is an error. All modes of behavior, of any sort, can be programmed and automated. It is a matter of breaking the behavior down into its constituent elements, into actemes, and then computing them back together again. Just such breaking down and recalculating is what programming is. The commandment mentioned earlier can be broken down into actemes such as "feed your bedridden mother rice pudding." Apparatuses will obey this commandment better, more quickly, and more precisely than human beings do.

The second hesitation to be optimistic weighs more heavily. It is concerned that freeing people from the obligation to behave in particular ways will result in a complete lack of freedom. If there is no necessity to act in a particular way (to work, to walk, to sit, to calculate, to draw), then all behavior will revert to an *acte gratuit,* a meaningless, absurd gesture. This objection assumes that freedom can open up only in the struggle against necessity. Completely unconditioned behavior is no more free than completely conditioned behavior. At this point, an optimist might object that any human behavior, whether compliant with instructions, is absurd in the face of death (the inevitability of death) and that the underlying intention of all instruction was always to give this absurdity a meaning. When instructions are shifted from human beings to apparatuses, human beings are free to give meaning to the absurd behavior of apparatuses (and in so doing, to their own behavior as a function of the apparatuses). Accordingly, to program is to give meaning, and the intention behind programming is to free human beings to give the world meaning and to make their lives in it free.

Maintaining an optimism that dispels our fear of programming, one could claim that with the demise of writing through programming, the goal of history is achieved. All behavior has become profane, scientific, functional, apolitical, and people are free to give such behavior meaning. History, and the mode of thought that produces history, is over. A new, posthistorical mode of thought is arising that assigns meaning to absurdity. Let us leave aside the question whether this optimism actually satisfies all conditions. Even if we do accept it, the question whether programming will render all writing obsolete remains open. All instructions can be programmed, but things other than instructions will be written. Literature does not consist wholly of commandments, laws, and user's manuals, after all. And these other threads in the literary mesh may well not be programmable. So writing will continue after all. And by means of this sustained writing, historical, political, ethical, and aesthetic modes of thought will be preserved.

This (reactionary) objection proves to be an error. It is true that literature does not consist exclusively of instruction, of models of behavior. There are also models of knowledge (e.g., scientific and philosophical texts) and models of experience (e.g., poetry and everything understood by belles lettres). Dividing literature into models for behavior, knowledge, and experience follows the classical division of ideals into good, true, and beautiful, a division that has been insupportable since the Industrial Revolution. Today we have a way of reducing models of knowledge and experience to models of behavior by tracing all propositions back to *if–then* propositions. Propositional calculus permits all statements of whatever kind to be translated into functions. All literature becomes programmable.

A programmed literature would take all texts back to instructions so as to then be computed by artificial intelligences. Even judging by the synthetic images that are already available now, it is clear that exceptionally effective models of knowledge and experience can be produced in this way. As binarily, digitally coded models of knowledge illuminate the screen, from simple statistical curves to complex representations of whole theories, they put all scientific, alphanumerically coded texts in the shade. So-called computer art is just beginning to generate models of experience (fantastic, impossible configurations) that are in fact images, but images that rely on digitally coded programs that are themselves transcodings of alphanumerically coded texts. These remarkably powerful models of experience should be seen in the first instance as programmed poetry and fiction, and only then as "visual art." In this way, an optimistic perspective on the programming of all writing seems justified: if alphabetic writing is to be replaced by digital programming, then all the messages, texts, behavior, knowledge, and experience that were once mediated by texts will be transmitted more effectively and more creatively through the new informatic media.

But we should not let ourselves be swept up by this optimism. Much would be gained by the programming of everything that has been written alphanumerically until now, but the terror of reactionaries cannot be dismissed so lightly. For in the recoding from alphanumeric into digital codes, something would be lost that not only reactionaries may acknowledge as the critical value of writing. For spoken language would lose its position as mediator between thinking and writing. Digital codes are ideographic in the sense of making concepts (ideas) visible. They differ from the alphabet in signifying no spoken sounds. In programming what was formerly alphabetically written, thought will have detached itself from language. And that is terrifying.

Writing, as we learned it in school, is a gesture of historical consciousness. Programming, as our children are beginning to learn it, is a gesture of a different sort, a gesture better compared to a mathematical than to a literary consciousness. The codes it uses are as ideographic as numbers. Wittgenstein, in his remark on the meaninglessness of saying "two and two is four at six o'clock in the afternoon," showed that mathematical thought is unhistorical. But until now, mathematical thought has been organically immersed in alphanumeric code and swept along in the flow of historical thought. Now programming is rising up from alphanumeric code, becoming independent and separating itself from spoken language. That justifies a degree of pessimism.

Spoken Languages

When programming has set itself free of alphanumeric writing, thought will no longer need to work through a spoken language to become visible. The detour through language to the sign, such a distinguishing mark of Western cultures (and all other alphabetic cultures), will become superfluous. Thought and speech will no longer be fused, as they were when the alphabet was predominant. This fusion is the reason the rules of thinking are called "logic" (rules of words), that we use language criticism as a method of analyzing thought, that the Bible claims the Word to have been the beginning, or that Heidegger calls words the "house of being." This fusion of thinking and speaking is actually remarkable. For there certainly have always been other codes besides the alphabet for making thought visible, for example, codes of painting and codes of mathematics. So people were always aware that speaking was only one of the ways to play with thought, and they repeatedly attempted to find a common denominator among them. An impressive example is the (failed) effort to reduce the rules of logic and of mathematics to one another (see Russell and Whitehead, *Principia Mathematica*). But the alphabet was the dominant code. For thousands of years, it overshadowed all others. As the alphabet is surpassed, thought will liberate itself from speech, and other, nonlinguistic thought (mathematical and pictorial, and presumably completely new ones as well) will expand in ways we cannot yet anticipate.

Speaking, on the other hand, will not be surpassed at all. On the contrary: released from the alphabet, spoken language will flood the scene, tapes and speaking images will scream and whisper to society. Even artificial intelligences will learn to speak. There will be technical developments in speech, the skill of perceiving spoken language. The danger will be that language, released from the alphabet, will revert to an uncultivated state. Our languages have passed through the filtering and caustic grid of the alphabet for thousands of years, and in this way, they have become powerful and beautiful, delicate and precise instruments. If they are allowed to grow unchecked, they—along with a great deal of thinking—will become barbaric.

The alphabet's effect on speaking should not be overestimated, however. For in observing the contemporary linguistic situation, one notices that the overwhelming majority of writing and speech is nonsense and worse. About 95 percent of everything spoken and written is grammatically incorrect (say, such statements as "this washing machine is better" or "Berlin lies in the north") and for this reason actually says nothing. After listening to people in the street and reading the flood of newspapers, magazines, and novels, a glance at a computer program can come as an aesthetic refreshment. If this twaddle, this demagoguery, ceases to dominate thinking after the loss of the alphabet, it might be regarded as an epistemological, political, and aesthetic catharsis.

Language is certainly a high intellectual achievement, and the languages available to us belong to our greatest treasures. Some of the innumerable aspects of this legacy that have been left to us to preserve and expand are sketched in what follows.

Our languages (the Indo-Germanic and Hamito-Semitic) are inflected; that is, in them, words change meaning according to their position in the sentence order. Sentences formed from such words are pro-nouncements: predicates pushed out by their subjects. Accordingly, the things our languages say (the universe of our languages) consist of projectile, arrow-shaped situations. For example, the sentence "Hansel loves Gretel" is a sketch of "loves" that goes out from Hansel and aims at Gretel. This is not true of all types of languages. In agglutinative languages (e.g., Tupi-Guarani), there are word collages instead of sentences so that their universe (that of which they speak) has a circumstantial rather than a projectile character. In some isolating languages (say, in Chinese), there are no sentences, but there are juxtapositions of syllables, and instead of a projectile character, their universe therefore has a mosaic character. So long as we think in ways bound up with language, we will be disoriented in these two universes. They make our thought unsteady because they offer evidence that our universe is structured not by reality but by our languages. So the unsteadiness is a good thing, but it also shows what we owe our languages: they offer us the net in whose threads and knots we think, feel, desire, and act.

All our languages have the same inflected character (although German, for example, tends toward agglutination, as in *Donaudampfschiffarhtskapitän* [Danube-steam-ship-journey-captain] and English toward isolations, such as "put" or "set"). But each of our languages manipulates this structure in its own unique way. Each has its own grammar. That enables us to relocate from our own language into another without falling out of the net that supports us. And translation is a powerful method of expanding and deepening our universe. For our languages are open systems: elements of other languages (words and rules) may be incorporated without loss of character. Translation enables us to say something we've said before in our own language differently. The variety, the structural similarity, and the functional difference among our languages means our universe is always open to a creative renewing of ideas, feelings, desires, and acts.

This variation in our languages has one more aspect. Spoken languages are acoustic phenomena. Each language has its own melody and distinctive rhythm, and this on multiple levels: from that of phonemes to the level of words and sentences and from there to the level of discourse. Many of these linguistic melodies and rhythms converge (e.g., the musicality of Italian with that of Russian), whereas others face off against each other (e.g., the rhythm of Czech with that of French). As a result, we are in a position to create linguistic compositions and to continually bring new resonances to our universe.

Our languages are codes in which various wordings are locked into symbols for concepts, and the rules of sentence construction are locked into rules for thinking. They are double-locked codes. Now codes tend toward two opposed horizons, toward denotation, where each single symbol means one particular element in its universe, and toward connotation, where each symbol refers to a region of that universe that is ambiguously defined, and each element in the universe may be referred to by more than one symbol. The advantage of a denotative code (e.g., symbolic logic) is that it is clear and distinct; that of a connotative code (e.g., painting) is the wealth of references and resulting variety of possible interpretations. The double locking of our languages means they can be expanded toward both horizons. We can speak exactly and precisely (denotatively) as well as allusively and suggestively. We can even do both at the same time. Our languages are exceptionally productive codes as a result. Our universe is an exceptionally rich one.

Our languages are youthful creatures compared to the age of the species "man." Indo-Germanic and Hamito-Semitic languages appear to have a common root that doesn't reach back very far into the Neolithic. But human beings have probably been speaking for hundreds of thousands of years. So our languages are systems that have hardly been deployed at all so far and that could be deployed in untold ways. And yet the experience of hundreds of generations is stored in our word forms and sentence construction. When we speak, this collective memory presses from us out into the public arena, where it is enriched. This is not the case for all spoken languages. Most languages—the so-called primitive ones—are not sufficiently codified to serve as memory. In some Indian languages, the vocabulary changes from decade to decade because many words become taboo and may no longer be used. Some other languages are by contrast so highly codified that they seize up and can no longer be developed (ancient Egyptian would offer an example). We face the challenge of preserving and passing on our languages' precious balance between rigor and elasticity.

The enthusiasm for our languages that has been expressed here explains the pessimism with which the last chapter closed. For if the future brings a new code that relies less and less on linguistic codes and more and more on codes of calculation and computation, if the swell of speech that will then flood over us turns out to be no more than background noise for the new mode of thought, then we may well fear the loss of language, the precious legacy we have abandoned. We may comfort ourselves with the thought that before the invention of the alphabet, spoken language as a unique code was continually enriched and transmitted, and that the same might happen after the alphabet becomes obsolete. But this does not diminish the fear. For with respect to spoken language, prealphabetic conditions are categorically different from postalphabetic ones.

Prior to the invention of the alphabet, spoken language was (to the extent we can establish it in retrospect) a carrier of myths, that is, of models of social experience, knowledge, and behavior. And there were people, the mythagogues (probably predominantly the old and wise), whose task it was to pass the myths on. With the task came the further responsibility of preserving and enriching the languages, a duty that was taken over by alphabetic writing. Homer may be an example of the transition from speaking to writing as a language-preserving and language-creating gesture. (The mythagogues were probably singers, incidentally, so that the transition to alphabetic writing could have been perceived as an impoverishment of a whole dimension of spoken language.) After the alphabet becomes obsolete, there will no longer be an elite entrusted with the preservation and enrichment of spoken language. Left to itself (that is, to prattle), language will run wild. A glance at the current situation, though still embryonic, shows how little hope there is that an illiterate elite of the future might take care of the language.

Certain phenomena seem to signal the formation of such an elite. Let us consider two of them: the books spoken on cassette and oral poetry on cassettes and records. Both examples were identified because they represent extreme cases. Spoken books are texts read aloud so that the spoken language depends on what has been written alphabetically, whereas oral poetry specifically rejects any transmission through writing. The first example can be provisionally bracketed out of this discussion: if no more books are written, there will be no spoken books either. Such communication without images would be an unnecessary impoverishment of the message. The second example does deserve attention. Here the new mythagogues (Dylan Thomas, Brazilians, Indian and African bards) seem to have a creative effect on language and to restore its lost musical dimension. Not until the invention of the tape recorder, one would think, had linguistic creativity had such an immediate and extensive impact as with these poems distributed in their millions. But are we actually dealing with poetry? However one defines this word etymologically—whether as dictation or as adage—on closer consideration, there is something different going on with these new mythagogues.

For cassettes and records are largely obsolete. Not so much because an opera on videotape carries more information than one on a record but rather because images suit the rising new mode of thought better than sound. For this reason, poetry on cassettes or records will soon be displaced by video clips. That is just a question of the rapidly diminishing costs of the requisite apparatus. Poets who are still making cassettes and records will program video clips, not only because they are not actually poets (engaged with language) but also because they create new models of experience. They address those who cannot yet afford clips. Their linguistic creativity serves a rising technology, and the speaking and singing images they will produce—in fact, already produce—will use language among more prominent codes. And so exactly because contemporary spoken poetry is so creative, it shows that spoken language is doomed to enter the service of new codes and to become background noise—as we know it from sound film, in music, and still more in speaking as an auxiliary function, so that it can be said of silent film that it is the true filmic language.

In the postalphabetic situation there will be no elite entrusted with the care of language. People will be subject to persuasion from all sides, and it will penetrate into them more deeply than ever before, but in terms of effect, speaking will merely assist (as, say, gestural codes do today) the dominant codes. This suggests that with the rise of speech in an unimaginably distant past, a rich and creative gestural code was degraded into something auxiliary, just as speech is about to be degraded. That justifies pessimism. In the future, people will speak as Neapolitans gesticulate. Considering the treasure that language is, that is a misfortune.

Poetry

A distinction is traditionally made between poetry and mimicry (poiesis and mimesis). But under the sway of the alphabet, this close connection between thinking and language—poetry—is usually understood as a language game whose strategy is to creatively enlarge the universe of languages. This universe becomes poetically broader and deeper through the manipulation of words and sentences, the modulation of linguistic functions, a game with the meanings of words and sentences, rhythmic and melodic modulation of phonemes. Poetry in this sense is that source from which language always springs anew and, in fact, overall in literature, even in scientific, philosophical, or political texts, not only in poetic ones. The preceding reflections imply that poetry, as the opposite of imitation, will break new ground, in fact, ground that only opens with the introduction of apparatuses and the codes that go with them. Images will detach themselves from their imitative, mimetic function and become inventive and poetic. This poetic power is already clearly visible in films, videos, and synthetic images. As for poetry, in the sense of a language game, on the other hand, its route to the new culture appears to be blocked: for it is bound to alphabetic writing.

At first glance, it looks as though there could also be nonalphabetic language games. Can't apparatuses play with language just as well as with images and musical sounds? Could there not be electronic poetry along with electronic images and electronic music? It's possible to think of programs that produce linguistic modulations automatically that could far surpass alphabetic modulation in poetic force. Such programming could liberate alphabetic poetry from the elitist prison it occupies today and, mindful of the decaying alphabet, lead to finer, stronger speech. Should this strategy be employed, we could expect psalms and epics such as those of David and Homer to be brought to a new level. A new song to the Lord would then be at hand.

To detach poetry as a language game from the alphabet and to transpose it to computing apparatuses assumes that there are people engaged in strengthening and honing the language. This is exactly what the previous chapter put into question. To forecast future poetic activity, we must reflect on poetry as the opposite of imitation to then look closely at the special case of poetry as a creator of language.

We are not always aware of what we owe to poetry in the broader sense: almost everything we perceive and experience. Poetry produces models of experience, and without such models, we would scarcely be able to perceive anything. We would be anesthetized and would—having to rely on our atrophied instincts—stagger about blind, deaf, and numb. Poets are our organs of perception. We see, hear, taste, and smell on the basis of models we have from poets. The world appears for us through these models. Poets created these models. They did not just work from raw, shapeless material they found somewhere: if we see colors, then it is through van Gogh and Kodak; if we hear sounds, then it is through Bach and Rock; if we taste, then it is through Brillat-Savarin and fast food. These colors, sounds, and tastes are as they are not because they come to us naturally but because they have been culturally—that is to say, poetically—shaped from some imperceptible natural ground.

Let us attempt a history of perception on the hypothetical assumption that colors were perceived differently before and after van Gogh. It would be a history of aesthetics, of experience. Let us choose the experience of love.

In our contemporary experience of love, we recognize models

of love made in Hollywood, shaped from those of romantic poetry that in turn was shaped from those of the troubadours. Behind these models, we find Christian love models, and behind this, Jewish and Greek love models, until the roots are lost in prehistory. Within this genealogical tree of love models, we can confirm such offshoots as the *eros* of Plato, the *Amor intellectualis* of Spinoza, or the *Amor fati* of Nietzsche. This historical view leads to a kind of aesthetic Darwinism. Our own experience of love is related to that of the ancient Greeks as a mammalian ear is related to a fish's gills or the Toltecs' experience of love as a mammal's eye to an insect's eye. Here the Hollywood models appear to be the most recent and highest limb of a linear development: aesthetic imperialism. We perceive better and experience better than any older or so-called underdeveloped cultures. What we perceive to be true is the truest of all.

Given that we know how models are produced, how poetry is made, namely, through the computation of existing models with intrusive noise, such a history of perception is no longer tenable. We have before us not a branching genealogical tree but so many compartmentalized models that proliferate in all directions, with links between single models running through them. We should speak not of progress but of multiplicity in perception, not of a history of aesthetics but of a complex system of aesthetic models. That our lives are conducted according to only a few experiential models should be interpreted not historically (or by implication politically, as a victory of the stronger over the weaker) but cybernetically.

The model of love that channels the contemporary love experience is Hollywood's rather than the Buddhist or the central African because media channels are built on an historic, imperialistic pattern. When this pattern becomes obsolete, these channels can be reordered. If cable were introduced to the media, for example, central African love models could be transmitted as well as those of Hollywood. No historical revolution (resistance of the weak against the strong) is needed for such a reordering. It is already happening because the media demand cross-connections on the basis of their inherent communicological[1] structure. And that is why a great many models of perceptions that had been suppressed until now are pushing their way into the channels that feed us. We already perceive in a far more complex manner than earlier generations did. Not only our love lives, but also our perceptions of color, sound, and taste are becoming more complex. Poetry in the sense of a construction of experiential models is already beginning to develop now and will achieve dimensions in the near future that will exceed all expectations. What all we will perceive and experience in the future is unimaginable.

The discussion was about sounding and moving images. Of course, it is possible to consider spoken languages in this context and say that poetry in the narrower sense, poetry as language game, will also undergo a powerful development, thanks to the cross-connections in media in the form of speaking images. We could then anticipate a new poetic creativity, not only in images and music but in language as well. But so detached from the alphabet, wasn't everything we treasured about poetry lost?

The alphabetic poet manipulates words and linguistic rules by means of letters to produce a model of experience for others. In doing so, he thinks he has forced his own, concrete experience (sensibility, idea, desire) into the language and so made this experience and the language that has been changed by this experience accessible to others. The new poet, equipped with apparatuses and dining on them digitally, cannot be so naive. He knows he has to calculate his experience, to dissect it into atoms of experience to be able to program it digitally. And in making this calculation, he must confirm the extent to which others previously modeled his experience. He no longer identifies himself as author but rather as remixer. Even the language he manipulates no longer seems like raw material stacked up inside him but rather like a complex system pressing in around him to be remixed. His attitude to a poem is no longer that of the inspired and intuitive poet but that of an information designer. He relies on theories and no longer works empirically.

Such an informatic approach to poetry has long been in preparation. In Mallarmé, for example, this attitude finds theoretical, nearly informatic expression; and the cool, calculating, exact, even mechanical dimension of poetry is clearly visible in the precision of many of Shakespeare's sonnets. One could almost say that poetry matures as it abandons its empirical, intuitive attitude in favor of a theoretical one. Except that with the abandonment of the alphabet, poetry loses all its naivety. All our conceptions of poets favored by the muse must yield to a conception of the poet as a language technician. Poetry will be desanctified.

Two comments should be made at this point, however. First, a reflection on the transition from oral to alphabetic poetry is in order, in particular, the way this transition is personified for us in the figure of Homer. Didn't people at that time speak in the same way about the technologizing and desanctifying of poetry as they compared the inspired singing of the bards with the literate poet's manipulation of letters? Second, we should question the detachment of the calculating poet. The new poet, sitting at his terminal and waiting expectantly to see which unanticipated word and sentence formations appear on the screen, is gripped by a creative delirium no less intense than the one a writing poet felt in his struggle with language. Each time a technical threshold is crossed, observers have the sense that technology is getting the upper hand, and each time, it turns out that the new technology opens new creative possibilities.

So it looks as though intuition will give way to calculation after poetry becomes informatic. But really, it is about a displacement of the poet's intentions. The alphabetic poet set out to change the rules and repertoire of a language according to a prior design. He saw the poem to be written in his mind's eye, and he tried to force the language to do justice to the vision. The calculating poet turns the rules and repertoire of the language into a game of random permutations, and his intention is to select the most suitable ones from these computations that arise at random. This new level of intentional play with chance is what distinguishes the new poetry from alphabetic poetry.

We would accordingly expect two kinds of poetry in the sense of a language game. On one hand, there will be artificial intelligences that speak, presenting a continuous program of new poems in keeping with their programs. And on the other hand, information designers will, with the help of a permutation game, cause poems—coded alphabetically or not—to light up on our screens before us at a breathtaking pace, like some kind of artificial Eliot or Rilke. Of course, it will also be possible to connect the bards to the Rilkes, assuming there are still people who are interested in language games. In light of the unimaginable number of perceptual and experiential models that will flood over society in the form of image and sound, it is doubtful whether language, by then forming no more than a background code, will still be used to model perception and experience. The forces of poetry will then probably be concentrating on nonlinguistic codes, some of them still unknown. Such codes will no longer be read but will have to be decoded in another way. This raises the now unavoidable question of the future of reading.

A poet writing alphabetically directs his lines toward a reader. He constructs an experiential model for people who presumably read to the end before starting to live in accordance with it. That means that the poet who writes alphabetically writes above all and in the first instance to critics. The new poet is not facing such an audience. The models he builds are to be received, changed, and sent on. He is playing a permutation game that he received from earlier poets and that he will pass on to future poets. In the future, there will be no criticism in the traditional sense of the word.

What we fear, as we anticipate the most perfect form and the end of alphabetic writing, is the decline of reading, that is, of critical decoding. We fear that in the future, all messages, especially models of perception and experience, will be taken in uncritically, that the informatic revolution could turn people into receivers who remix messages uncritically, that is, into robots.

Ways of Reading

Common sense (known to be untrustworthy) suggests that writing precedes reading, for to be able to read, one must have something written. That is incorrect. There was reading (e.g., of peas) long before the invention of writing. Writing itself is just a way of reading: it involves selecting written signs from a heap, like peas, to be strung into lines. *To read (legere, legein)* means "to pick out, to peck." This pecking activity is called "election," the capacity to do it, "intelligence." And the result of pecking is called "elegance" and "elite." Writers are not the first intellectuals but only the intellectuals characteristic of a particular historical period. They peck more elegantly than before. Assuming that reading precedes writing, and pecking precedes stringing (and so calculating computing), then we are facing difficulties common sense covers up.

Intelligence is the capacity to pick something out from a mass. Our prehuman ancestors were intelligent beings as they read fleas from one another's pelts. Hens, too, are intelligent: they peck kernels of corn from heaps. There are two methods of reading: according to criteria (knowing what to pick) or unselectively. The first method is called "critical"; the second is what the English word *to read* means—"to guess." Hens are critical. They peck according to the criterion edible–inedible. But such a criterion poses a problem for hens when it comes to writing. They eat the kernels instead of threading them. Our prehuman ancestors may, on the other hand, have arranged the selected fleas in rows before they ate them. The setting of stones in rows argues in favor of such a conclusion and suggests—uncomfortably—that critical thinking came before writing. Those who claim that writing initiates and promotes our critical faculties (an argument of this book as well) must try to adjust their position to account for the hens.

Not everything can be pecked. There are illegible things. But everything can be picked apart so that it can be pecked. It depends on how sharp the picking beak is, and science hones the beak finer and finer. But one hesitates before this formulation of the theory of perception on which science is based. The beak needs to pick apart to be able to peck later. If the beak becomes finer and finer, then the kernels it can eventually peck will have to be smaller and smaller until they can't be pecked anymore. If science has calculated everything down into kernels that it can no longer peck, then the world has become illegible again. Criticism, which precedes reading and is meant to make reading possible, can become too exact and so prevent reading. That, too, is uncomfortable. It appears to leave things illegible, mysterious—despite our having seen the capacity to be critical as the root of human dignity since Kant at the latest.

To read critically (e.g., the way hens distinguish between kernels of corn and kernels of sand) is to evaluate. Corn is good; sand is not good. If *interpretation* has something to do with *pretium* (price and/or value), then hens interpret. The opposite of critical reading is puzzle solving *(to read)*. This is not about the pecking of the proverbial blind hen, who, of course, is known to find a kernel now and then but is rather about a way of reading that categorically rejects evaluation. Science claims to read in this way. It claims that as far as it's concerned, a kernel of sand has the same value as a kernel of corn, and both may be pecked in equal quantities. And science goes a step further, claiming that the puzzle-solving mode of reading represents an advance over the critical mode. To leave values behind and approach symptoms, a disciplined way would be the ideal way to read. Cultural sciences, in interpreting the phenomena they select, are imperfect sciences compared to natural sciences, which refuse to interpret phenomena. That, too, is uncomfortable. For it would seem that the critical faculty—far from being the basis of human dignity—is more characteristic of hens than of people. The claim of natural science must be picked apart.

In their natural state, people were omnivores. They read every-thing around them and in them interpretively: trees and dreams, stars and coffee grounds, the flight of birds and their own livers. They evaluated and priced all of it. Then, hesitantly and one step at a time, they learned to read symptoms. They progressively re-moved all the price tags from phenomena and fitted out the heap of peckable kernels with value-free numbers instead. In fact, this price tag removing progressed from the outer reaches of the world closer and closer to the center, toward the readers themselves. First the price tags were removed from stones and stars. In this way, the first value-free sciences of astronomy and mechanics were established. Then came the devaluation of kernels in the forms of chemistry, biology, sociology, psychology, and so on, closer and closer to a human being, until finally, puzzle-solving, value-free reading penetrated into the most secret corners of our thoughts, feelings, and desires, driving out all values, all interpretations. The hard science of symptomatology is about to eliminate all soft interpretation from the legible world. There is nothing to criticize in a world that has become value-free. No one is holy and no one is criminal if he can be read as holy and/or criminal because he acted under the influence of an ill wind and/or because he couldn't sleep with his mother.

If reading symptoms is the only right way to read at all, and all interpretive, evaluative reading is seen to be primitive, gallinaceous, reading in general can be turned over to artificial intelligences. They are less like hens than we are. They don't keep slipping into evaluations; they are simply stricter. As far as we are concerned, we can give up reading and learning to read. And along with reading, we can give up writing—this reading that threads letters into lines.

How is critical reading actually different from reading symp-toms, solving puzzles? From a heap of kernels that are to be read, the critical reading picks out the good kernels until the only ones in the heap are not good. For puzzle-solving reading, there are no good or not good kernels, but even this way of reading must peck some of the kernels and leave the rest. Puzzle-solving reading, too, must stand before two heaps in the end, perhaps before one heap of large and another of small kernels. Large and small are in fact not values (but quantities), not price tags (but numbers), but there must be some criterion for distinguishing between large and small. There actually is such a criterion. It is called a "standard." A kernel is large or small in comparison to a standard. This standard is calibrated, that is, equipped with a zero point from which all other points are established. So puzzle-solving reading reveals itself to be critical reading in disguise. Its criterion is a zero. The hard sciences are not value free but rather order all values in relation to an absolute zero. For them, the statement that a kernel is large (or good or beautiful) in and of itself makes no sense; rather it must be described as relatively large.

So interest shifts to this absolute zero. Let us call it something positive to get to the bottom of all this measuring in the hard sciences. Let us call this zero "truth." It is a zero point because it means an extreme position, unattainable and therefore empty. In this context, it does not present any great difficulty. Whether truth is something that eventually manifests itself, something we finally uncover, or something we keep trying to achieve on the basis of *adequatio intellectus ad rem* (the adaptation of the beak to the heap of kernels), it is always at an unattainable borderline. A puzzle-solving reader is attracted to this borderline. Popper calls it "falsifying": one pecks at the heap of false kernels until (at the end of time) only the true kernels are left. And behold: truth is unattainable, but somehow it must have been there all the time. Otherwise, how could the false kernels have been recognized as false and read out of the heap? The puzzle-solving reader reveals himself to be just as primitive as the reader who uses criteria: like the hens, scientists know from the start which kernels to peck.

The salient point here is Newton's sentence *hypotheses non fingo*

(I feign no hypotheses). The verb *to feign* (to behave as if) has three substantives, namely, *fiction, figure,* and *feint.* Newton means that his hypotheses are not fictions. But he must admit that they are figures meant to assist in sifting out the truth once and for all, and that they are feints, like all other figures such as parables, hyperboles, allegories, similes, and metaphors. Puzzle-solving reading, unwilling to assume any prior values of any kind, nevertheless has a fictive character. So Leonardo came to speak of *fantasia essata,* a fiction of precision.

The assertions of science are on shaky ground. The puzzle-solving way of reading is a criterion-setting one in disguise, and science establishes values just as politics and art do. Science, like art and politics, is a fiction. It is becoming more and more clear that it is nonsense to try to distinguish sharply between science, art, and politics. We can assume that in science, there are normative-political as well as fictional, artistic, and poetic impulses at work, and that in art and politics, the search for truth continues. In the future, we must learn not to distinguish between value-free reading (science) and interpretive reading (art and politics). We must see, with Rilke, that it is an error to distinguish too strictly. If we learn to do this, we can expect surprises. What science, art, and politics will draw out of us, once they are bound into a unified way of reading, will exceed our wildest dreams.

The uncomfortable aspect of this by now unavoidable merging of science with art and politics is, of course, that it will shortly become impossible to distinguish between fictional and nonfictional. If science has shown itself to be one fiction among others, then it no longer makes sense to speak of "real" reality: "real" is what the fictions say when they speak to us. That is surely what Nietzsche meant with his assertion that art is better than truth. If puzzle-solving reading, shown to be a criterion-bound reading in disguise, is lost, with it goes our capacity to criticize, and here we surely mean knowing the difference between fiction and truth. We will then have seen through critical reading and will no longer be able to criticize. The basis of all critical reading is exposed as a belief that cannot be criticized.

Hens believe that corn kernels are good. Science makes this belief relative: corn kernels are good in relation to eating (and sand kernels in relation to the beach). That rests on the scientific belief that reality is value free. To approach this belief critically is to realize that reality is as we believe it to be. And this third belief can no longer be criticized. For now it is clear that to be able to criticize what is there, another belief must come into play. Only on the basis of some kind of belief is reading possible. All critical reading must start from a belief that is not open to criticism. Without it, nothing can be criticized, nothing is legible. We have lost this uncritical belief. With it, we've lost the capacity to criticize and to read at all. It makes no sense to learn to read and write. There is nothing more to read and even less to write.

The puzzle-solving reading that science endorses as the alternative to interpretive, critical reading has shown itself to be critical reading in disguise. This shatters the foundation of reading, namely, the belief in legibility (unconditional decoding). Yet it is still possible to find within this crisis an entirely different kind of reading and to go on reading in the future. Until now, *to read* was understood to be the unraveling of a mystery. Wittgenstein rightly points out that there is no longer anything to unravel. Having lost our faith, we are actually incapable of recognizing a mystery in the world or in ourselves that can be read and resolved. But it is also possible to translate *to read* as "to guess," and rather than mystery, one might have a montage game—a jigsaw puzzle—in mind. So *to read* could mean to peck and assemble kernels in such a way that something meaningful is produced. This new way of reading is beginning to crystallize now. It is called, of course, "computing."

It is characteristic of computing to assume that the world and we are meaningless (absurd), that either can be picked into kernels, and that the kernels can then be assembled into something that does have meaning. The calculating way of reading lends meaning to a meaningless original text. We are dealing with a reversal of the vectors of meaning: no longer does the reader draw a meaning from what is read; rather he is the one who confers meaning on what is read. To this new reader (and to artificial intelligences), there is nothing out there or in here that means anything at all: there is nothing behind it. The only meaning to be derived from the whole nonsense will be that projected through peckable, assembled mosaics, selected from particles out there and in here (e.g., synthesized images). The mosaics are fictions, figures, feints; in the aftermath of the antiquated ways of reading, they are the only reality we will have in which to live.

With this, all criticism has reached its original goal, the Enlightenment is everywhere victorious, and there is nothing more to criticize or illuminate. Everything has become clear, above all that all criteria, values, and measurements are ideological and that nothing stands behind these ways of reading (appearances). A fully enlightened consciousness no longer needs to be intelligent, to be about extracting meaning. It can concentrate on creative amalgamation. This transition from the old ways of reading to the new involves a leap from historical, evaluative, political consciousness into a consciousness that is cybernetic and playful, that confers meaning. This will be the consciousness that reads in the future.

Deciphering

The word *cipher* comes from the Arabic *sifr* (empty). The words *chiffre* and *zero* are derivatives as well. It was the Arabs who introduced us to numbers—and above all to zero. It is not necessary to understand set theory to know that numbers are empty containers meant to peck out quantities of something. For example, the cipher "2" is an empty container for pecking pairs, and the cipher "a" is an empty container for pecking any number of specific spoken sounds. The difference between "2" and "a" can be found only in that from which they peck: "2" pecks from a set of ideas (is an ideogram), and "a" pecks from a set of spoken sounds. Pieces of writing, texts, are rows of ciphers, whether they are letters or other written signs, and to read them means to de-cipher them, that is, to peck out the quantities (the contents) the ciphers contain. Writing pecks contents by means of ciphers, and reading pecks out again what has been pecked in. That is what encoding and decoding mean. One takes the nominalist view in supposing that numbers, types, and universals are purely conventions and that the kernels could be pecked in containers of any form at all. Numbers just happen to be convenient containers. The problematic aspect of this view and its reappearance now, after centuries of "realist" hegemony, has already been discussed at an earlier point in this essay.

Numbers are not simply lying around us like teaspoons or bowls; rather they are ordered in a system, exactly because for pecking kernels, it is important to have special containers for special types of kernels. Such numerical systems have rules governing the relationships between numbers. These systems are called "codes."

One speaks, for example, of the alphabetic code and of the code of Arabic numerals, and when these two codes are combined, one can speak of an alphanumeric code. The word *code* comes from the Latin *caudex,* meaning "tree trunk." The word *book,* too, came from the name of a tree. Letters are ciphers of a code.

Before reading a piece of writing, one must know what code it uses. One must decode it first, before one starts to decipher it. That is not always an easy matter. For example, the scribblings near and below the cave paintings at Lascaux were recognized as codes only with the aid of computers, and the traces left by rain on a mountain near Rio de Janeiro were long thought to be in code (phonetic letters). A Martian fallen to earth would conclude, based on the strange regularity of irregularities in the distribution of ciphers in any given phenomenon—that is, with the help of information theory—that he was dealing with some kind of codified message. Computers are such Martians come to earth. Champollion, who unlocked hieroglyphic code, was a computer avant la lettre. But all this is unnecessary in everyday reading. We received the key to alphanumeric code in our schoolbags. We can confine ourselves to the deciphering of texts.

Deciphering is pecking out the contents from their containers; it is an unfolding of that which the encoder put in, folded in, implied. And this not only at the level of single ciphers but at all levels of the encoded message. Should these contents be folded strongly (as, say, in the fragments of Heraclitus or in Wittgenstein's *Tractatus*), then deciphering is a strenuous activity. But usually, our eyes fly along the lines and pick up the contents easily; that is, as we know, an error. For in this way, not only can many hidden contents, sitting deep inside the container, get past us, but also, and worse, we can be letting the encoder lead us down the garden path. For he can give an *A* for an *O,* he can lie, and attentive deciphering will catch him out. That shows that there are various ways of deciphering, at least the following: the careful unfolding, the hasty once-over, and the mistrustful sniffing about. The first could be called the "commenting," the second the "obedient," and the third the "critical" sort of deciphering, in the awareness that any deciphering requires that the reader have a critical attitude: he must have criteria to recognize ciphers as such and then to decipher them. The sniffing sort of deciphering is called "critical" because in it the critical attitude takes on the character of a method.

Pieces of writing are directed at the decoder. The writer reaches his hand out toward the other to reach a decoder. His political gesture of writing goes out not to people in general but to take hold of a decoder. As a result, decoding and encoding, reading and writing, should be divided into the categories suggested earlier. There are texts that intend to be commented on. Others are to be obeyed, and still others are to be criticized. There are not many categories that classify literature better than these. But they are hardly ever actually used because they address literature from the standpoint of the writer rather than from the standpoint of the reader. The reader can justifiably ignore or mistrust the writer's intention. He can obey texts that demand commentary (e.g., scientific ones), obey those that demand criticism (e.g., poetic ones), and criticize any kind of text whatsoever. If his text remains unread, perhaps even more forcefully: if his text is deciphered incorrectly with respect to his intention, the tragic aspect of writing comes into view—the writer feels cornered. This is why the destiny that is his text persecutes him with fear and loathing—although with helpless concern as well. For he can do nothing more than wait passively to see whether his text will find a decoder to read it correctly. This addresses an aspect of all intersubjective connections, but one that is especially clear with writing.

1. *To comment:* The word means "to think together," inasmuch as *mens* can be translated into English as "think." The concept of "mind" or "mente" is missing. It corresponds to the gesture of writing, this gesture that produces something half made in the expectation of being completed, that is, commented on, by

a reader; that the reader should think with the writer to think through what has been thought, to lengthen the lines of the text to a conclusion. The Bible springs to mind as an example of commentarial reading, the Talmud as an even more impressive one, on whose pages sequential commentaries surround the object—the biblical text—in concentric circles. On a page of the Talmud, the destiny of a text is made visible. But the example also shows how commentary serves to render a text banal, to profane (spread out) the text message. The biblical sentence "honor the Sabbath, to keep it holy" (a formulation already profaned through translation) has received so much commentary that its contents have been emptied, and so exhausted. The text has been written down and spoken away. This, too, is a tragic aspect of writing: writing seeks commentary, and when it is successful, that which has been written is eroded away to banalities.

2. *To obey:* In principle, only texts that transmit models of conduct (*should* propositions) expect to be obeyed. The problem with instructions is that, on one hand, all *should* propositions can be translated into *if–then* propositions, and on the other hand, that all statements, whether they are indicative models of knowledge or optative models of experience, contain a hidden grain of obligation. We know, for example, that the obligation hidden in the indicative statements "the earth rotates around the sun" and "the sun rotates around the earth" was contested to the point that a life was sacrificed (Giordano Bruno). Whether a text is deciphered as a should proposition depends at least as much on the reader's intention as on the writer's. It is actually amusing to watch scientific texts being twisted into rules of conduct through "scientistic" reading. Such obedient reading, turning scientists into unwilling authorities, comes from the linear construction of texts. The eye must follow the line to receive the message. In this way, all writers become authors and authorities, whether they want to or not. Faith in the text, that

sly form of slavery, can lead to monstrous contortions, however. For an obedient reading of a text need not be a quick flyover; it may be a slow crawl along each line. With such crawling, all levels of a text except the absolutely literal one are lost to the reader. Faith in letters (e.g., in some kabbalistic practices and in some religious and political movements) shows the extreme edge of such obedient reading, namely, the danger of textual idolatry that lurks in writing of any kind. Those who fear a totalitarianism of images need to consider this murderous textual totalitarianism as well.

3. *To criticize:* The words *critique* and *criminal* come from the Greek *krinein* and the Latin *cernere,* which mean something like "break" in the sense of "break apart" or "break the law." We have known these double meanings at least since the Enlightenment (and especially since Kant), as it became clear that the one criticized saw the critic as a criminal, as did the critic the criticized. To read a text critically is to take the writer to be criminal and to commit a crime against him. The whole thing is steeped in a criminal ambience. The reader becomes a detective or a murderer, and it can happen—as in some detective fiction—that the detective is the murderer. The writer is always a criminal because he always lies, even if he is not aware of it. The critical reader suspects him by reading against the lines, into him, into his context, into his unconscious. So he discovers that what the writer holds to be true is actually class ideology, a sublimation or some other objectively demonstrable prejudice. The critical reader can further discover that the writer lies consciously. Such deciphering is especially successful with newspaper texts that count on obedient, uncritical reading and so can lie with impunity. The critical reader is always a criminal because he does not grasp the arm that has been extended to him in brotherly way but rather pushes forward along this arm toward the writer, to take him apart. Many writers nevertheless search for such a critique because

it is the way they discover what was going on inside them as they wrote. Ideally, they would like to get commentary and criticism simultaneously, but that is an impossible demand. For commentary proceeds from the text outward, and criticism penetrates into and through it. The history of the Enlightenment could be described as the progress of this penetration: at the beginning, the Enlightenment advanced against texts (in Kant's case, against scientific and philosophical texts; in Rousseau's, against political and aesthetic ones), then it penetrated into writers (e.g., with Marx or Freud), and finally, as for example in the Frankfurt School, into a confused massacre to end all lies by means of lies. In this sense, too, critical reading, the Enlightenment, can be seen as having ended successfully. All texts, even critical ones, have become critically decipherable, and all lines are turned against themselves, like Ouroboros, to swallow their own tails.

There are two basic reasons to write: the private motivation (to put one's thoughts in order) and a political one (to inform others). Today we are sufficiently enlightened to call these motives to account. The ordering of ideas is a mechanical process, attributable in any case to the order of writing, and can be left to artificial intelligences. The readers to whom one writes are commentators (who wear away what has been written) or followers (who subject themselves to it like objects) or critics (who tear it apart), should readers be found at all. So the feeling that writing is absurd, which seizes and gnaws away at many writers, cannot be attributed to superficial matters like textual inflation or the rise of more suitable codes alone. It is rather the result of becoming conscious of writing as engagement and as an expressive gesture. A glance not only at the cultural scene but above all into himself shows the writer that his hour has begun to strike.

An example of this depressed mood is the following. As I type, I try to do two things: to put my ideas concerning the fall of writing in order and to share them with others. I know, however, with a certainty bordering on probability that in ordering my ideas, I have made mistakes that would have been corrected had I programmed them into a computer. And I know with certainty how my text will be read, should it be read despite text inflation. It will, namely, be spoken away, or it will be passed over, or it will be possible to show that I lied, consciously or unconsciously. What is the case for what has been written here is also the case for the example just conceived in the course of writing: Ouroboros. And I wrote it nevertheless. This "nevertheless" stands as an invisible title over all texts written today.

And why should writers actually complain? They are, after all, readers first, before they become writers, if reading comes before writing biographically as well as ontologically. Everything written comments in answer to hastily and critically read texts. It is finally the reader who hides writings in various ways. When the writer as reader hides the writing of others, it is hardly surprising that he, once enlightened, also hides his own writings—even as they are being written. He has just learned how to decode his own coding. What remains are empty containers. Once we know that to write is to draw all zeros, the word *cipher* has won back its original dreary meaning.

A reflection on writing and reading cannot rest at such a zero point. If it doesn't work this way, one must try another.

Books

This written reflection on writing, this "superscript," has unwill-ingly arrived at the conclusion that we should expect writing to decline—for reasons that converge from various directions on this conclusion. This bundle of reasons can be summarized as follows: a new consciousness is coming into being. To express and transmit itself, it has developed codes that are not alphanumeric and has recognized the gesture of writing as an absurd act and so something from which to be free. The question arises whether we are forced to accept this unwelcome conclusion or whether it is still possible to avoid it. We are, in fact, concerned that with the decline of writ-ing, the critical faculty will also be lost. Whether this motivation is justified (whether our continued engagement with writing is rational, whether criticism is linked to writing, or whether it is a desirable way of thinking at all), the motivation is strong enough to start these considerations again. Not the gesture of writing but the concrete actuality of writing will be the starting point.

If writing were to be abandoned, packing paper would be the only kind of paper left. Overcome with homesickness, cellulose would withdraw back into its cells, forests would flourish, and reeds would sway in the morning wind, not only on the banks of the Nile but in all the waters of the world. Doesn't this green utopia fill us bookworms, termites who chew through paper, with sheer horror?

By then, there will be artificial memories different from and better than libraries, to be sure. Everything that was once stored in libraries will be transferred into these new memories. The contents of the *Encyclopaedia Britannica* will take up less than a cubic centimeter of space, and any information it contains will be instantly available at the press of a key. There will be apparatuses that make any piece information one wants light up the screen as a sounding image, that test it from various angles automatically and follow its logical consequences. All this testing and following will then be automatically fed back into the cubic centimeter encyclopedia. It will grow of its own accord, without being more than a tiny fragment of the information stored in the artificial memory. This, along with the green forests and the reeds swaying in the wind, should be cause for joy rather than horror.

But high-function automatic memories, on one hand, and green forests, on the other, are for us paper people places to visit, not to live. We inhabit paper, we are used to it, and because it is so familiar, so ordinary, we have made it sacred so as to be able to perceive it at all under cover of its familiarity. *Bible,* for example, comes from the Greek *byblos,* which is the way the Greeks pronounced *papyrus.* We have been chewing paper for so many millennia that this papier-mâché, saturated with our spittle, has become a part of our being. Without paper, we would no longer properly be there and so couldn't set out on journeys to the lands of green forests or artificial memories. Paper is that substrate that absorbs all our knowledge and experience, be it the adventurous new signs of artificial memories or the green blur of the forests. We suspect that whatever cannot be put on paper may not be anything at all. Paper is our home, even if this home threatens to flood over us like a raging sea. One might say, then, that the informatic revolution would save more than the forests. It would save us from the danger of being inundated with paper. But we're bookworms, and we eat the very thing that is eating us. We live from books and for books.

A book is, from one point of view, an intermediate stage on the way from the forest into the land of artificial intelligences. It is always some part of a forest: *book* is a tree name; *liber* is tree bark and comes from the Greek *lepis* (shell), which in turn derives from the ancient *lep* (to peel). The book was peeled from the forest, and its leaves say what they say. But the book is also a piece of artificial intelligence, for it is an artificial support for memory consisting of bits (letters) of computed information. The book may be seen as what one must go through to get to artificial intelligences (even if this passage took a few millennia). But we don't see the book in this way at all. We don't think of it as it was peeled out of the Egyptian reeds and rolled up, as having been folded, cut, sewn, and bound to be dissolved finally in the aforementioned cubic centimeter. We don't see these things in it because it turns its back on us. It doesn't turn its back silently or with contempt but with an attractive and promising gesture. It carries seduction on its back. It wants to be turned around, opened up, and paged through. These three movements, to which a book's spine seduces us, can't be done with trees or artificial intelligences. They are characteristic of the intermediary stage between the two. What we gained by leaving the forest, and what will be taken away from us again, is turning around, opening up, and paging through.

Turning Around

The wall of a library is fundamentally different from all other walls. Walls are arrangements for distinguishing between public and private space. Walls facilitate vital decisions, for human life oscillates between public and private. A human being inhabits a back wall and experiences a front wall. Walls must be set up to allow for oscillation. There are openings to be made (doors) for going out and coming back in; others (windows) through which publicity may be desired in private and through which the private is publicly inspected. And pictures are to be put on the walls to hold on to that which has been seen and experienced. Whether television and computer screens are to be regarded as windows or pictures, there is no difficulty fitting them into the structure and function of the wall. We are dealing with technically developed walls, in which the window and picture functions overtake and suspend one another dialectically, making the doors superfluous.

But the wall of the library is different and functions differently. The spines of the books, lined up beside one another and over one another, form a secondary wall, positioned in front of the actual wall. Between the spines of the books and the actual wall is a zone of paper, where, in consideration of the reflections just undertaken here, numerous arms are trying to take hold of us. They can only do this if we ourselves stretch out an arm in their direction, pull a spine out from the wall, and turn the book around, to allow ourselves to be taken in by it.

Turning around is a synonym for *revolution*. Two things happen with the pulling out and turning over of the book. First, the actual wall becomes visible behind the book that has been pulled out. Second, the arm of another, stretched out toward us, can be grasped. *Revolution* surely means to become aware of the walls that separate us, to be able to take hold of the other (be it a stranglehold, an intellectual grasp, or a mutual holding of interest).

Revolutions raise two questions: for what and against what? Usually, the answer to the question of against what is easier to give. It is clear in the case of turning the book over: against walls. In the case of the scientific revolution, it was clear: the walls of science, their paradigms, were to be uncovered so as to be broken through. In fundamental revolutions, for example, in the industrial or the current informatic revolution, the walls cannot be recognized so clearly. Even less clear is the "for what" of the revolution. It does not help very much to pay attention to the revolutionaries' stated intentions because they themselves can't conceive of the "for what." The Russian revolutionaries didn't know that they would bring the present Soviet Union into being. With the turning over of a book, however, the "for what" of all revolutions becomes clear: for the other. To pull out and turn a book over can serve as a model revolutionary gesture.

No wall can be revolutionized except the library wall. It makes no sense to beat one's head against it. It is more reasonable to go through the door, to look through the window, or to hang pictures, for all others are outside and can only be reached there. The library wall, however, not only permits but even encourages the revolutionary gesture because the other is already inside. Only in the historical universe of the library wall are revolutions possible, not in that of technical images.

Opening Up

A book that has been pulled out and turned over is lying on the table to be opened up. Here one is faced with a different kind of choice from the one that decided on one book among others. The choice of one among many books challenges choice itself because it becomes clear that the choice can only be made from a limited quantity, and that in light of the library wall having become gigantic and incomprehensible, one grasps without choosing—either taking one's luck or directed by criteria unrelated to books (perhaps more on this decline in representative democracy later). In the choice of opening up, on the other hand, there are four methods. One opens to the table of contents or to the index, looks for pictures, or doesn't open at all but rather pages through. This last method, which actually avoids the choice, will be singled out for discussion.

One opens to the table of contents to determine what the book is about. One grasps the arm of the other not for his sake but for the content's sake. This detached opening sees the book as a treatise "about." When one reads it, one stands above the matter so as to be able to treat it from high to low. It is not quite right to want to grasp the contents-page-opening reader statistically. How many of us take the trouble to climb over the subject matter so as to dive into it again from above?

One opens to the index to determine what company the author keeps. Not only the names, but the things, too, show this, for they are things a society shares. One grasps the arm of the other to participate in his society. This intersubjective opening sees the book as part of a dialogue and an invitation to take part in it. Many books, including this one, have no such index,[1] not necessarily because they are refusing the reader but because they refuse to align themselves in a society. So the absence of such an index is irritation and a challenge to someone who opens a book in this way: he is irritated because he doesn't know with whom he is dealing, and he is challenged to recognize the other, whose arm he is grasping, as an other (rather than being able to locate him). Should this challenge be accepted, a new dialogue may arise instead of a continuation of one that had already begun.

One opens to illustrations to get an idea about what should have been grasped at the outset. A decent person does this with a guilty conscience, for he knows that the illustrations were put into the book so that they would be seen as a function of the writing. That bad conscience is a symptom of a troubled sense of history: prehistoric images are preferable to those integrated into a text. Here, too, a statistic would be helpful: how many of us open books in this way (like children and other illiterates), and do they do it out of the remaining fragments of a prehistoric consciousness or out of the new consciousness that is currently arising? Books without illustrations are those that transmit concepts that either can't be represented or that don't wish to be represented. These books either can't be illustrated or someone doesn't want them to be.

Opening up a book is a gesture that makes a choice about the way the book in question is to be read. Now it is possible to get help with this (e.g., card files, and adopting the technology developed for artificial memories, opening apparatuses as well as abstract services, information and documentation centers, etc.) so that the actual choice in library practice need not take place in front of the wall but is taken over by the wall itself. The ability to choose is an important aspect of freedom. The revolution of turning the book over should be followed by the choice of how to open it. Artificial memories do not open books up, and even old books start to withdraw from the choice. This can be seen as a symptom of the decline of representative democracy.

Paging Through

Freedom includes the ability to choose, and the necessity to choose shows a lack of freedom presenting itself as freedom. Two borderline cases disavow this: the one in which the choice is impossible because of inadequate criteria (such as incomprehensible quantities) and the one in which all alternatives have the same value (Buridan's donkey). So not being able to choose is an important aspect of freedom as well. Leaving things to chance is about freedom. This is about the gesture of paging through.

If one lets the pages of the book run through one's fingers, it is in the expectation of accidentally stumbling on a way to find the loose end of a thread the book spins. There is something labyrinthine about this search for the end of an Ariadnian thread.

In analyzing the probability, one finds a series of reasons— among them distinctive letter forms—that are designed to make the paging person "accidentally" stop. In analyzing the reasons, however, one finds a series of coincidences behind them, for example, that the distinctive letter forms were pecked on a whim by the author or typesetter from the available letter forms. The layers of chance and causation, this sandwich structure of all explanation, has the effect of making the pages the reason for a specific way of reading, according to which the book is to be decoded, just like the various methods of opening the book. (That is just what is meant by the saying that chaos is unexplained order and order is unexplained chaos.)

There is no paging through truly artificial memories.

Should books be replaced by memories that function better, there will be far cleverer methods of getting a look at the information stored in them than paging through. A whole science and technology concerned with such methods is emerging. It would make no sense to try, say, to turn these memories around—unless one were a specialist charged with repairing possible damage. But as for revolutions by specialists, there are none. The low-function possibility of turning around, choosing, or leaving things to chance, the low-function historical freedom, would be lost. We are bookworms, beings opposed to automated apparatuses and green forests, not out of bibliophilia—which today registers as necrophilia—but out of an engagement with historical freedom. This, our "wormlike feeling," this sense of nourishing ourselves on corpses (books), explains our horror of dispensing with books.

Letters

The German word *Brief* (letter) means "short writing" (French: *brevet*) and in English "short written summary." But it is no longer used in German with this meaning. There are long *Briefs*. The reference is to texts that are not intended for the public, not directed to a publisher—even though many letters have been published, and many more, apparently directed to a specific addressee, are really eyeing up a publisher.

In the previous chapter, the era of writing appeared as a transitional stage on the route between the forest and the land of automated apparatuses. In this context, letters, too, are just transitional manifestations between sounds reverberating in the forest and those we hear in a robotic automobile when we forget to fasten the seatbelt. Even now, their transitional status is unmistakable. For example, at a time before writing, "in time of suffering you should call me" meant one should scream to God. In historical times, there were written commandments for this purpose, and today one thinks first of the telephone, even knowing it will be impossible to find the right number in the directory.

It is curious that the telephone, this first instance of cable networking, has not displaced the postal service. So in the French PTT,[1] *P* remains the first letter and *T* the last. That will change as soon as the telephone is telematically linked to computers. This, as we are beginning to realize, need not lead to central nationalization but can lead to decentralized privatization (see the United States and Japan). Yet it is still true that the postal system is currently just as overburdened as the telephone network (and Minitel as well, first introduced in France, the first inkling of telematics). There must be something about writing letters—and reading letters—that allows both to stay afloat.

I don't know whether anyone has written a postal philosophy. It would have to start from an analysis of waiting. Letters are things one waits for—or they arrive unexpectedly. Of course, waiting is a religious category: it means hoping. The post office is founded on the principle of hope. Postal carriers, these functionaries who seem practically medieval, are angels (from *angeloi*, "messages"), and what they carry are evangels (good news, with respect to the hope that sustains the post office). It can't be said that all hope would be lost if the post office disappeared. Telephone calls are awaited with fear and loathing as well, and if it rings unexpectedly, the telephone is a lightning strike from a clear sky. But expecting a letter has a different duration and a different rhythm. Letters may be expected for weeks, and this expectation intensifies at specific hours of the day. What has just been said describes the duration and rhythm of celebrations. Perhaps the letter has barely kept its head above water because it offers one of the very few elements of celebration we have left. This reflection on correspondence starts at this point: a letter as a piece of writing in honor of someone or something.

Like everything concerning celebrations, letters follow established rituals. For example, a letter carries a return address (often printed), a so-called date with an indication of the place and day of completion, the address of the one to whom the letter is directed, and a formal greeting to the addressee. A letter closes with an equally formalized farewell and is signed. Each one of these forms can be justified, for each has a rational function within the goal the letter is pursuing. The same is true of all rituals: Jewish food rituals, for example, can be justified as hygienic measures. But that kind of explanation misses the crucial point, namely, that we are dealing with absurd gestures. The absurdity becomes evident in imagining someone addressing another person orally with "dear sir" or ending a conversation with "best regards."

A study of correspondence rituals from an historical, geographical, or sociocultural perspective (to say nothing of others) would make a valuable contribution to our knowledge of society. In comparing contemporary flourishes with those of the Baroque, English with French, or those of a business letter with those of a love letter, one would be looking at formal, not to say structural, social criteria. Letters involve a certain solemnity that is in fact catholic (all participate) but whose ritual is appropriate to the social position of the celebrant. These rituals are plastic as well: a celebrant has a number of nuanced formulae available and can shape them himself. The contemporary reform of church rituals is far from having attained the catholicity and plasticity of letter-writing rituals.

So it becomes clear that writing letters is closely related to writing poetry. In addition to the rules of grammar and orthography, the writer of letters is charged with others (such as the verse form of rhyme pattern in poetry), and these supplementary rules are festive: at once justifiable and absurd, both rigid and flexible. That leaves the writer with two strategies open to him: first, the classic, in which the writer is concerned with a structured whole, produced according to the rules and by means of the rules; second, the romantic, in which he is concerned with a relaxation and creative extension of the rules. The pendulum between classic and romantic, this dynamic of poetry (and from there to art in general), and this as much in an historical as in an individual sense, is characteristic of letter writing. It is for this reason to be regarded as one of the most refined of the arts.

It is in decline. There have been times of full bloom, as, say the late Roman, the Hebrew "response literature," the eighteenth century. And the current time of decline is not the first. But it has a new character. This is not about the decline of the art of letter writing, this is about a decline in art in the traditional sense, about a decline in writing altogether, about a loss of the disposition to celebrate.

Letters are sealed and thrown into black boxes (painted yellow, red, or blue), to be drawn out of black boxes somewhere else (e.g., post boxes) and opened. The whole process is a secret, steeped in epistolary secrecy. Hermes, messenger of the gods, is, in fact, the winged angel that watches over the post office. The hermeneutic of the postal service is analogous to that of all black boxes and can be broken down cybernetically. Along with other spheres (such as the atmosphere and the biosphere), the earth has a postal sphere, a network of letter channels that is becoming more and more dense. But the postal sphere cannot be regarded as a closed system (as can, say, the biosphere). It nourishes itself on plants pounded into paper, on human beings who write characters, and on plucked birds—when people were still writing with quills. Because it is not a closed system, entropy is not a threat, but its sources could dry up. The felling of the Amazon forest threatens the postal sphere as much as the decline of alphanumeric code. In anticipation of this possible collapse of its sources, the postal sphere merged with those of telegraphy and telephony to form PTT. But these are both different kinds of spheres. Unlike oceangoing ships, earthbound trains and automobiles, or airborne airplanes, they are no longer supported by the earth. They run, by contrast, through unsupported electromagnetic fields. The connection with TT tears the *P* away from the earth—and so out of its secret.

The postal link that spans the earth (like the link of freemasonry) tries in vain to accommodate itself to this separation from the earth, but in vain, because it (like the Freemasons) is archaic by its very nature. All its avatars notwithstanding, it looks like the Roman couriers who hurried from military post to military post and the postilion who entered the medieval village with a blast from his horn. Looking more closely, it's possible to recognize troubadours, those poets who rushed from town to town. But it is exactly the archaic aspect of the postal service, these archaic gestures of sealing and seal breaking, that explains the attraction it continues to exert. We are at the point of jumping off the earth, physically and even more mentally, of leaving everything chthonic, everything that rests on mother earth behind. We therefore long to return to the great mother earth, the womb of the cave, the secret hidden behind seven seals, to the Eleusinian mysteries whose last form is the postal service.

Kierkegaard described the way letters are received, anxiously awaited, or unexpectedly appear, spit out of the postal carrier's great pouch. First they are decoded, like all other texts. Then they are read between the lines. Kierkegaard means that they are read in the same way as the Bible, that letter of all letters. And if they are not read in this way, they are not Bibles. Any text can be read like a letter, that is, not critically, but in an attempt to recognize the sender. Of course, the recognition can turn into criticism if the letter turns out to be a lie. The letter models the highest form of any textual reading.

We possess images that enable us to visualize the reading of letters: those of the Annunciation of the Immaculate Conception. The messenger is the archangel Gabriel, and the receiver is the Virgin. We latecomers interpret Maria's surprised, hesitant demeanor as a reaction to the hidden angelic phallus that will introduce the *logos spermatikos* to the virgin. Theology insists that this is about a symbolic rather than a physiological event, however. The angel is carrying a letter, not a phallus. Mary draws back because she is being told to read the letter and then to provide the word *(logos)* with a body. Mohammed must have been just as shocked when the same archangel began to dictate the Koran to him (God had to try it twice because the post doesn't always work properly, as we know). What is happening with Mary, with Mohammed, and with the receipt of letters in general is the opening of the self to another, who becomes manifest from out of a hermetic secrecy.

That can no longer be achieved given the current conditions of the postal service. What becomes manifest from secrecy today is largely advertisements (in the form of disingenuous letters) and bills to pay, that is, letters that contain unarticulated threats. Advertisements are to be thrown away without breaking the seal, and bills are to be made to disappear as quickly as possible. There is the occasional genuine letter in this unholy flood of paper, but in most cases, they turn out to be about matters that resolve themselves of their own accord, given some time. Today the postal service no longer facilitates an opening but rather a closing against the other, no longer an immaculate conception but rather one soiled with protective measures, a conception by preservative. Not only is it impossible to read all texts as though they were letters; it has also become just as impossible to read letters differently from texts that are subject to criticism.

The festivity of letters, their religious ambience, depends on their secrecy, this mysterious sealing with which we cast a letter into the opening in the hermetic system. That is religious, for it is faith in the postal service and trust in it that cause us to entrust it with our secret. In the meantime, we've learned that we are wise to approach the postal service with a measure of doubt. No seal, however it works, can keep a secret. The profane light of public enlightenment permeates all things locked and sealed, for the cave of secrecy has developed cracks. The interests of transparency, the public, the "someone" has cracked its way into all things private, dark, and unexplained. "Someone" in the shape of a censor is pressing through the cracks into the secrecy of the letter. A letter is no longer directed toward an intended other only but unwillingly also toward an intruder who appears, faceless, in the undifferentiated mist of "someone." The faceless intruder actually obscures the faces of those who willingly recognize one another: festivity is not absurd; it has become contradictory.

Letters are writings not intended for public access that nevertheless can find their way, by means of a censor, into an anonymous public sphere. The postal service is secret, a black box that has developed cracks. Nets that don't need to be supported from the ground but that can hover without support have become carriers of intersubjective messages. The festivity and secrecy of letter writing and letter reading dissolve. The existential attitude of waiting, attending, anticipating has become superfluous with respect to the global simultaneity of messages transmitted electromagnetically. To hope is no longer to anticipate but to be surprised. It no longer makes any sense to write letters.

To the extent that teletypes and, later, higher-function telematic media took the place of letters and the postal service, we can see what we are losing with the piece of paper called a "letter": one of the last openings through which we could hope to recognize another. For however the telematic message is decoded, and however it is answered, it will not be read between the lines. We have a new form of festivity, a new form of secret, a new form of mutual recognition, and it is so completely unanticipated and unexpected that we are too surprised to be able to recognize the letter in it. We are forgetting the art of letter writing and have not yet learned the art of inter-subjectivity, computer art. The letter is being withdrawn from us (by one who is faceless but wears various masks), and we are falling into an unstructured mass; still we suspect that the mass media are beginning to branch out into intersubjective, letterlike media. This dull suspicion alone, for which the word *hope* is too strong, enables us to witness the demise of letters and the postal service.

A dull suspicion is beginning to take shape, and this in the form of a money order. A check is a letter directed to a bank, directing it to give money to the bearer. Today there are plastic cards fitted with artificial memories instead. Perhaps this intelligent bank card is a harbinger of all future letters. It is possible that letters, unlike books, will make the leap into the informatic situation and that letters will survive writing. A look into the future: an earth encased in intelligent plastic cards that whir about like bees, spinning human relationships like threads of honey with an inaudible hum. By then, we paper-boring termites would have turned into honey-licking inhabitants of cells. An assessment of this development must be left to those who still have access to values, or who act as though they do.

Newspapers

A vast literature concerned with newspapers, along with innumerable schools of journalism scattered around the earth, debate the curious fact that despite television, radio, and until recently, weekly news programs, there are still folded fliers that are flown into our homes daily. Or they wait with folded wings every day in specially constructed cages for us to fall into the trap. It cannot be only because newsprint is suitable packing paper—an inadequate explanation for two reasons: first, because better packing material is available, and pieces of meat wrapped in newspaper seem as antiquated as bridle paths; second, the explanation is not elegant enough to be taken seriously. So are newspapers as antiquated as bridle paths, even though they keep using improved technology, even though their characteristic writing style changes in response to the latest information and communication theory, and even though their information is governed by increasingly refined systems of production and marketing? Specialists in the study of newspapers put forward far more complex and probing explanations for the persistence of printed newspapers, even as they justify and forecast a ubiquitous electromagnetization of information.

These complex and probing explanations (which will not be pursued here) change nothing about the fact that there shouldn't be any newspapers anymore. But there is a banal explanation for their not having disappeared: although they appear to have saved themselves, unchanged, from the flood of electromagnetized information, they have, in fact, turned into the exact opposite of what they once were. Before radio and other media, the newspaper was an ephemeral, temporary, and quickly outdated memory in comparison to all other media (books, magazines, etc.). It was consigned to being forgotten. Nothing was so past and out of date as yesterday's newspaper. Later the newspaper became a durable memory in comparison to the new media, and this was the case even though it lagged chronologically behind that seen on screens and heard on speakers. In fact, this, too, can be stored elsewhere more safely on audio- and videotapes, but for the time being, these new memories are not passed in massive quantities from senders to receivers. They are jammed up somewhere, waiting patiently for suitable distribution channels. Newspapers do not compete with radio or television but rather with such storage tapes. The surprising thing is not that there are newspapers but that there is such a traffic jam in the media. It is worth considering a changed newspaper, one provisionally transformed into audio- and videotape.

It is a question of duration. "Duration" is a category to be distinguished from "time." Since electromagnetization, a newspaper might better be called a "lasting paper." The content of the newspaper is supposed to last somewhat longer that the content broadcast on radio or television; it should remain in the receiver's present a bit longer. Electromagnetic senders beam out roughly the same messages as the newspaper, but because they have no substrate (they're immaterial), they run uninterrupted though time, without stopping in the present. The receiver is required to absorb the message into memory as time is passing so as to store it there and process it later. The newspaper, on the other hand, is an artificial memory and allows itself to be handled, crumpled, cut apart—in short, to be grasped. It doesn't demand so much of the receiver's memory. So paper, which is an ephemeral memory in comparison to marble or metal, becomes a durable one in the context of electromagnetic media—until tapes and records take over this role.

The concept of "duration" points beyond time in the direction of that *nunc stans* (the abiding Now) that is related to eternity. Some of those who write for the newspaper may be aware that it has become a "lasting paper," a message pointing in the direction of the eternal, but few if any of those who read it will realize this. For the receivers, the newspaper has retained the character of a flyer. It flies over them. The division that has developed in this way between many writers' attitudes toward the newspaper and those of most readers raises a more significant question about the sustainability of newspapers than does the competition with electromagnetic senders. To provisionally bridge this gap, the layout (the superficial aspect of the news page) tries to visually separate the durable segments from the others, in the hope that a few readers of texts so designated as durable may treat them differently (e.g., cut them out). In this way, an internal contradiction arises in the newspaper contents: one part points to the library, a larger one to the wastebasket. There are therefore two completely different types of writers for newspapers: the one writes for libraries, the other for the wastebasket. And the newspapers themselves can be classified into two groups according to this criterion: into the predominantly librarianish and the predominantly wastebasketish.

Formulating loosely, the wastebasketish group can be called "journalists" and the other "news staff." The first can be divided into employees and freelance journalists, the second into permanent and occasional. But it is still a mistake to consider such an attempt at classification to be evaluative, say, to place a higher value on staff members than on journalists (as is done by a tiny elite) or to value the journalists more highly than the staff members (as is done by most casual newspaper readers). The suggested classification of newspaper writing is value free, and that means it is indifferent to this sort of writing.

This indifference (the quality of being scientific) appears in crass contradiction to the heated engagement of both staff members and journalists. The engagement of staff, permanently employed writers, is easy to understand from the perspective of writing. These people have a historical consciousness. Through temporal activity, they want to enter into eternity, whether for their thinking or only for their name having been preserved in the newspaper. For them, the newspaper is a vehicle for getting out of time and into duration, taking countless readers along.

The engagement of journalists, on the other hand, writers conditioned to the wastebasket, cannot be understood from the perspective of writing. These are people who are prepared, in extreme circumstances, to risk their lives to see that, say, war reports get past a diversion through the newspaper into the wastebasket. They are prepared to give their lives not for something particular to them (whether this be ideas, feelings, values, or even just their own names) but for information. These journalists are the heroes of the coming information society, which has given up duration and for which time is no longer historically structured. A whole future mythology will condense around the heroic figure of the journalist, and we can already see how this mythology is to be programmed.

The newspaper staff writers with their historical consciousness are distinguished from book and letter writers only by the medium "newspaper." These are writers who try to reach out a hand to another to change the world together and to get along in it. Journalists are of another sort. In the nineteenth century, before the first electromagnetic media existed, they were, along with photographers, the first "informatic" people, individuals who helped to develop a new consciousness. This close relationship, this common intellectual ground between journalist and photographer, has been preserved in the newspaper. That is the inner basis for the coupling of picture and text in journalistic newspaper articles. But because of the tendency toward electromagnetization, the medium that best corresponds to the journalist's own existence is the radio, and even more, the television. Since the newspaper became durable, journalists' migration from the newspaper into the new media (where the heroes of the future are) has become more and more evident. The newspaper is more and more clearly becoming a playground for staff—a document, even, that can't be sustained in the long run. "Duration" doesn't suit the informatic situation.

It is an anachronism to speak of the newspapers, of the press, as a so-called fourth estate. In the nineteenth century—and even still in the first half of the twentieth century—such an assertion was not only justified but also prophetic. The press is—seen from the past—the fourth estate: it is the most recent addition to the three political powers (however one wants to name them). Seen from the future, it is the first: it is where it first became clear that power is located wherever information is produced and distributed. That is the explanation for the rise of complex newspaper conglomerates and newspaper polyps, whose slowly decaying corpses still pollute the atmosphere. Power is there, where information is generated, in a globally diffused jigsaw puzzle, as we've learned the meantime. One can speak of a power of the press today only with nostalgia. The press is no more than a preliminary to the work of contemporary decision-making centers.

Above all, we should notice that the press trades in inherited political categories, whereas contemporary decision-making centers must be grasped cybernetically. There are still newspapers that address one party and others that emphasize a position above or beneath parties without saying whom they do address. There are still critics who try, through the newspaper and beyond, to read a political opinion and incoherent interest behind it. The whole thing has a ghostly character with respect to the new power configuration. Decision-making centers have become automated. They intersect with one another in complex ways, and the decisions can no longer be grasped politically; they no longer function on the basis of interests; rather they function on the basis of other functions of apparatus. The press hides this because it is attached to political power in decline—to survive. If there were no more newspapers, only radio and television, the current depoliticization and cybernetization of power would emerge more clearly.

The press should not be regarded as a power but rather as a last attempt to keep the deposed powers alive. It is as though the deposed powers can still express themselves in the newspaper, although in reality, they have nothing more to say. Political broadcasts on television confirm this. There the political statement is absorbed into a new, informatic consciousness: politics as a question of image is a very inexact expression for it, and a videocast determines who our presidential candidates will be. The newspaper is a last refuge of the political, historical consciousness, and in this sense, it is reactionary, even and especially when it presents itself as progressive. It cannot be achieved, neither with progressive production methods nor with a progressive layout nor with progressive distribution methods nor with progressive contributions from progressive staff. The newspaper is reactionary because it is a piece of writing and so a product of historical consciousness. For this reason, it is impotent in the face of the emerging posthistorical situation.

The newspaper will disappear as soon as video- and audiotapes and records from electromagnetic senders flow, cheap and plentiful (perhaps free), into all homes to be stored in video and audio libraries. Many newspapers try to put themselves on videotapes and survive, no doubt above all to preserve any advertising still left to them, from which and for which they live. But this is only an excuse. Advertising can be absorbed effortlessly from electromagnetic senders. This confused rescue mission is actually about maintaining an active political consciousness after the demise of writing, for video newspapers are supposed to politicize, not depoliticize. That is a contradictory undertaking. Political consciousness expresses itself in alphanumeric code. Given its structure, it cannot be recoded into images and sounds without losing its essential feature: linearity, a writing forward from the past into the future.

With the newspaper, the last remaining bit of historical consciousness disappears—and with it historical freedom. An observer from Mars will notice how the battle for freedom in the nineteenth and the first half of the twentieth centuries concentrated on freedom of the press. Why is the freedom of newspaper writers actually so important for the existential freedom of people from all sorts of conditions and all sorts of actions? Because political freedom expresses itself in freedom of the press. It is regarded as the basis for existential freedom. That may sound false to the Martian. How, he might ask, when political freedom (whatever that might mean) veils the existential sort so that people are given political freedom ("given" above all by reading newspapers), while existentially they vegetate, completely conditioned and utterly aimless? The answer to this Martian question will determine our attitude toward the disappearance of newspapers.

If we regard political freedom as the basis for freedom as such, then we will be horrified to see the newspaper replaced by a cybernetically governed production and distribution of information. If we see in political freedom an ideological veiling of the existential, then the demise of the newspaper presents us with alternatives. When the newspaper, this last remaining vestige of criticism, has disappeared, either centrally positioned senders will program all knowledge, values, and experience, in which case, we will no longer be able to speak of freedom because the word itself would have no meaning, or, when the newspaper—this centrally radiating flyer— has disappeared, we will see a new, networked way of producing information, and it will become meaningful for the first time to speak of existential information.

Newspapers are pages that radiate out from a center. They are structurally fascistic. But within this fascistic structure, freedom of the press (and political freedom) found a voice. The disappearance of the newspaper is beyond question. The question is whether the fascistic structure of the newspaper will be transferred to the new media, possibly strengthened, or whether, with the disappearance of the newspaper, other, netlike circuits will appear. The question concerns freedom.

Stationeries

This is not about those shops that confront and seduce us through paper but rather about shops that sell writing materials, although even in stationery shops, we encounter the first sort of paper handlers. Stationery shops are of concern because after the decline of writing, they, too, will disappear from our environment. One might argue that stationery shops should not be singled out from all the others, that all shops are condemned to disappear with the decline of writing. Once information can be called down onto screens in private spaces, it will be possible to call down any goods that are still of interest over a cable from central distribution points so that all shops (and the city) will become redundant. But it is different with stationery shops. They will become superfluous as shops, but so will the things they have for sale. The informatic revolution is a political one: we are losing the city *(polis),* and it is a cultural revolution—we are losing the culture of writing.

The loss of a culture of writing can be observed in office stationeries. In addition to typewriters and even older writing tools, they carry more and more word processors, which are evidently geared toward replacement by higher-function artificial intelligences that no longer use any paper. The design of stationery stores buries paper rather than praising it. The most melancholy aspect of this burial is surely the typewriter. What we mourn is not, say, the rather paleotechnical keyboard or the malicious ink ribbon that continually jams but rather the alphanumeric memory. We welcome the new keyboards and the absence of messy ribbons. But the letters, Arabic numerals, and adventurous ideograms like §, &, or $, no longer beckon us, as if they were secretly in league with us, namely, in the league of alphanumeric code. That is regrettable.

How letters are stored in the brain's memory, and whether there is a specific part of the brain where they are stored, is unclear at the moment. The problem itself is awkward: was there a place for storing letters in the brain as *Homo sapiens sapiens* arose, and so was such a place in the genetic information from the time life on earth began? Or has the brain functioned this way for only three thousand years? Neither Darwinism nor Lamarckism has the solution to this problem (and it is apparently at our door). But the problem looks different with typewriters. There letters are stored according to the frequency with which they occur in relation to a particular written language so that the fingers can call comfortably on those that occur most frequently: applied information theory, long before this theory was formulated. The typewriter comments on a question in the theory of knowledge, about the dialectic between theory and practice.

Another dialectic is relevant here. To the extent that we type, the letters are stored in our brain. On an English or German typewriter, *ABCDE* becomes *QWERT.* As long as there have been typewriters, letters must have been dancing in our brains, and the choreography of that dance would surely provide an insight into an important aspect of our thinking. This dialectic between brain and typewriter (mediated by the eye and fingers) is such that a part of the typewriter has migrated into our brains and a part of our brains into the typewriter. With the typewriter, a part of our brain will be lost, or to say this more optimistically, one brain function will be free to do something else.

This raises the question of the boundaries of the subject with respect to the objective world (of the difference between the I and the not-I) with impressive clarity. It shows the many-layered gray area that lies between what seems to be the "ego-nucleus" and what seems to be the not-I. If I cut my fingernails, remove my appendix, amputate an arm, or replace all organs with artificial ones, has the boundary between the world and me moved as a result? And what happens in this respect if someone takes my pipe, my old suit, or even my house away? In the gray zone, it is impossible to distinguish ontologically between "my" body and "my" stuff at all: fingernails are further from the ego-nucleus than the pipe. The same is true, mutatis mutandis, for "my" memory as well. Fingernails are further from the ego-nucleus than the Shakespeare stored in my memory, although the nails appear to grow from the inside toward the outside and Shakespeare from the outside to the inside through the gray zone. When the typewriter disappears, something will fall from the gray zone. This something is very close to my ego-nucleus. Should this ego-nucleus prove to be a myth, namely, as the core of a gray zone that becomes denser at its center, then the disappearance of the typewriter should be regarded as an impoverishment of the ego as such. That is an aspect of the dread that seizes us when we reflect on the decline of writing.

Not all writers type, and many who do type also write by hand. They do not have the close relationship with the typewriter described earlier. Many people think one must learn to type (as one learns to swim), and there are typewriting and swimming schools that support this view. There are even professions for trained typewriting writers. Informatization is bringing an end to this nonsense, making clear that typing is about an automation (meaning internalization, me-ification) that turns writing into a gesture like walking and speaking, in that we forget whether we ever learned it.

Stationery stores also show that not all writers just type. In addition to typewriters, these stores also sell various kinds of fountain pens, and in addition to machine and carbon paper, other writing papers. As for the varieties of pens, some available for free, the range of colors is worth considering. It contradicts the essence of writing and recalls the practice of drawing, from which writing freed itself in a development of hundreds of years. Pens are archaic because they recall the stylus (French: *stylo*) and drawing. It becomes clear that the true writing consciousness corresponds best to the typewriter, as is the case, on another level, for print. Those who write by hand find themselves on the outskirts of writing culture, where calligraphy and graphology, these ways of reading that seem medieval, hold sway. Handwriting is closer to ancient manuscript fragments than to computer programs. That people still write by hand, despite print and typewriter, may be attributed to the stubborn intractability of habitual gestures. It suggests that out of stubbornness, the gesture of writing will persist, like a useless appendix, for a long time into the informatic situation—a small consolation.

More interesting than pencils, ballpoint pens, and fountain pens is the writing paper on offer at the stationeries. It comes loose, "endless," or in notebooks. Among these bound papers, those for making notes are particularly interesting. The words *note, notice,* and *notorious* come from *gnoscere* (to know). Notepads serve knowledge, and those who write in them are notaries. There are notepads that have the weeks, days, and hours of a coming year printed in them. They are designated with the word *calendar,* which is misleading, for with notepads, we are at the heart of historical consciousness. At the same time, there are calendars (colorful images for each month) that point away from historical consciousness and into mythical prehistory. In sharp contrast to such illustrated calendars, note calendars do not serve reflection or leisure but rather histori-cal activity, so it is more accurate to call them "agendas." The note calendar could serve as a model for all historical consciousness and historical knowledge that corresponds to writing.

A note calendar can be considered from three standpoints: the beginning, the middle, and the end of the year. From the beginning, one sees the structure of the year, the basis of all historical activity, which is to say, the temporal space of freedom and its boundaries. From the second standpoint, it is possible to project actions into the future, in the assumption that there is open space. From the third standpoint, two things become clear: projects crossed out and the history of the year. Taken together, these three standpoints reveal the internal contradiction in the historical concept of freedom and so, too, in that of historical knowledge. A view toward the future sees free space, a view toward the past sees conditions, and a view from within linear time sees possibilities and probabilities. So knowledge that looks back explains history causally, and prognosticating knowledge explains it teleologically. Things will happen as many want them to, but they happened as they had to. The note calendar shows the core of the contradiction: it permits no view from an extrahistorical present.

To read a note calendar at the end of the year is to read a biography. To read it from the end to the beginning (an adventure) is to see the world's resistance to one's plans in the form of accidents and conditions. Both appear against the same background, a printed grid. Once the note calendar is replaced by higher-functioning memories and more nuanced futurizations, once we call on computerized data rather than notes, the printed paper will disappear from view to make room for invisible programs. A newer concept of freedom will replace the historical one (or there won't be one), and instead of causal and teleological explanations, there will be functional ones (should it be necessary to explain anything). The drama of historical consciousness (its tragedy and comedy), as it becomes manifest in the note calendar, will give way to another way of life.

What is true of the note calendar is true of all notebooks. For the moment, they are all empty playgrounds of freedom that will, in the course of linear time, be filled with notorious conditions and accidents. If stationers become superfluous because notebooks have become superfluous, it will be superfluous to worry about this tragicomic contradiction.

In addition to typewriters and pens, besides printer paper and other writing paper, stationery stores carry other writing implements: clamps, folders, glue. Overall, they offer an insight into the universe of literature. Erasers, in particular, clarify the difference between nonliterate memory, texts, and computers with respect to a possible loss of information. Further reflections could perhaps show Freud's theory of repression to be prealphabetic: a typographical error that occurs as the result of a faulty performance can be typed over (it can be repressed), but it can also be erased. Given the limits established for this essay, however, it is advisable to resist such excursions into writing materials.

Writing paraphernalia migrates from the stationer's to my desk and from there into the wastebasket. The content of the wastebasket migrates into the rubbish, and from there into nature, to potentially migrate from there back into the stationer's as new writing material. But the return route from the wastebasket to the stationer's is unworldly and does not enter my writing consciousness. In a sense, it isn't right to speak of writing materials after the wastebasket stage. Even in the wastebasket, they no longer deserve the name. Real writing tools start life at the stationer's. They end with the transition from the desk into the wastebasket.

To write a biography of writing materials, these things that emerge in an absurd cycle from nature through culture and back into nature, would be to write about writing. For the concept "writing material" can be understood very broadly. It can embrace the whole of literate culture. A biography of literate culture (e.g., of Western history) would then appear as an arrow that starts at a stationer's somewhere and ends in a wastebasket now. And the segment in the underworld, the part of the absurd circle no one mentions, will only become visible behind the wastebasket, in the informatic situation. We are probably the first generation in a position to write Western history from the wastebasket. So we see, when we look into the future, only the waste behind our basket. Coming generations will have to climb out of the basket and survey the whole circus.

So far, the effort to grasp the stationery and its eventual disappearance from the standpoint of phenomenology has remained fragmentary. There will be no more neglecting the crucial thing about the stationery store, the point of it all, namely, the desk.

Desks

Before desks are compared with the apparatus that will come and replace them, it is advantageous to clear the slate. An empty table is more than just a plane: it is usually made of wood and supported by four legs or is some kind of simplified artificial beast of burden. It is, in addition, an unattainable ideal: one continually sets out to relieve it of its burden, to clear the table once and for all. And one is filled with envy noticing on television the vast and empty writing desks behind which sit those said to be powerful. Putting oneself in their place, one gains a new perspective on power and the desk. The German word *Macht,* meaning "power," is a substantive of the verb *mögen,* "to like or desire." Its equivalent in romance languages is the substantive of the verb "to be able." What would the powerful still want to or be able to do while they are sitting at an empty table? Do possibilities and potentialities burst out from them into emptiness? And don't these things become realities in just that organized chaos on the writing desk? After centuries of antiphenomenological discussion, a phenomenology of power would have to start by recognizing it as an assertion of possibilities that become real in resistance, that power is not something already real with which one must comply or against which one must struggle; rather power seeks resistance to become real in the first place. Deferral of resistance (e.g., the case of the empty desk) destroys power, and one need not be Gandhi to see it. The notion of an empty desk is sufficient.

It is the will to power that seduces us into the stationery to gather all sorts of writing materials, to continually replenish them and to fill our desk. It isn't a will to power in general, however, but to a very specific power, namely, to the so-called power of the pen. And even though different kinds of power have a whole classification of their own, this one is ordinarily contrasted with that of the sword. The power that radiates from the pen, the possibilities and potentialities it generates, have a specific structure, despite our not yet having a proper field theory for it. When there are iron filings in a magnet's force field, then we can see how this power is realized. Even if we are just as deeply submerged in pen power as electromagnetic power, we are still missing the relevant Einsteins, probably because ideological fields, in contrast to natural ones, were always unified ideologically before they were investigated separately. An example would be the Marxist attempt to refer all fields of power, including that of the pen, dialectically back to a foundational field (the economic base). Einstein, as we know, was not successful in reducing all fields in this way because the details of discoveries in diverse fields tended against doing so.

What seduces the writer to go into the writer's supply shop to seize the power of the pen has already been discussed in part in this essay, even though it did not achieve a proper field theory of pen power.

The will to straighten circles out into lines and, on the basis of these lines, to reach more lines seduces the writing into walking to the stationer's to seize the power of the pen. This essay suggests that the will to this specific power is realized in the form of Western culture and that the force field of the pen can be designated as the base of our society in this sense—without excluding the possibility that from other perspectives, other fields of power may constitute the base. The will to this specific power takes the writing desk as its starting point.

Chaos reigns on the average desk: papers, folders, clips, ashtrays, typewriters, telephone, and other things lie on it and are illuminated by a table lamp. There is no average desk, and any comprehensive chaos can only be in progress. The average desk is an abstraction from all desks, and any phenomenology of the desk must start from a concrete desk here and now, in an awareness of the presumption of wanting to equate this desk here and now with the average one.

Chaos means, provisionally, a situation whose structure is not yet clear or a situation that arises after the structure has become clear. In other words, we find chaos either where order has not yet been confirmed or where order has been completely confirmed.

The chaos on my desk is analogous to that in the universe of natural sciences. One who approaches unknowingly encounters messy confusion. Then he begins to confirm relationships, a method in the madness. When I sit at the desk and write, I am in a marvelous space: everything is in its place and at my service. I am then the Aristotle as well as the Newton of my desk: all writing instruments are in their assigned places and will, should they move, inevitably return there. With a knowledge of the table order, the locations of all writing instruments can be determined in the past, present, and future. But if I step back from myself and my desk and survey the convoluted relationship between it and myself, I become more and more Heisenbergian: what I regard as order on my desk reveals itself to be a gross simplification I myself have projected onto it. That becomes clear if I look for, say, a pin on it. Chaos reigns on my desk to this extent.

Now I seize power, which is to say I reach into the chaos, to put two pieces of paper and a sheet of carbon paper into the typewriter. My gaze is directed neither at the paper nor at the desk but rather past these to the text to be written. The whole writing desk is just a contemptible means to an end. It will be redeemed for some reason that is still nebulous for the moment. No seizure of power can avoid this redemption of the means. However, one can try to appreciate rather than despise the means. Only a strange confusion results: the more attention I pay to the paper and the typewriter, the more confused the intended piece of writing becomes. By looking at the desk, I squeeze the text out of my field of vision. This is why, when the powerless challenge the powerful to consider the means before using them, they are refused: the powerful are being asked to become impotent. And a glance directed at the table does in fact show the impotence and not the power of writing. The old saying "respice finem" no doubt means one ought always to keep death in mind, but it could also be interpreted as advice to look past the table: not to be inhibited by the means.

If I sit at my desk to look at it (rather than to write), it greets me coldly. There are two main reasons: because two implements antagonistic to writing are lying on it—namely, a telephone and a radio, two extraterrestrial invaders of the universe of writing—and because the power of the pen, aspiring to be a means of empowering unbridled "intellect," turns out to be in league with the malice of writing instruments.

In considering the two ETs on the desk, one gets the impression that we are dealing with two opposing ways informatization intrudes on writing. The radio provides background music and serves writing. When the telephone shrieks in its idiotically insistent way, it interrupts writing. So one could conclude that informatization can intrude idiotically and disturb writing but that it can also be enlisted successfully in the service of pen power. That is a false conclusion. The background music the radio delivers is not the white noise that serves to make the information produced in writing perceptible (communication theory discusses it); rather it mocks writing. It whispers in the writer's ear: the information you are producing is not directed to any reader after all but to my black box to be made into background music itself. And the insistently shrieking telephone doesn't interrupt writing, it stops it, saying: I am a new power of words, against which pen power struggles in vain.

The empty tables of powerful people we see on television carry batteries of telephones, whether we can see them or not. In the case of the very powerful, there is a red telephone among them.

The powerful sit at a desk to use telephones and not to write. This function is regarded as power. A Wittgensteinian question arises: what is the meaning of the sentence "that is a writing table, but it isn't used for writing"? The two ETs on the desk are inhibiting because they undermine both the power of the pen and the concept of power as such.

In turning one's attention to the other things on the desk, the definition of writing as the manipulation of symbols comes into question. Do I actually struggle against such soft things (software) as letters and the language they refer to when I write? Do I not have to contend above all with the intractable stubbornness of the torn ink ribbon, jammed controls, or hopelessly misplaced paper? You heavenly powers of the pen, you know no one who has not tasted the bread of tears (such as tears of frustration with a typewriter that no longer works). Literary criticism sees only what is heavenly, not what is earthly about writing, apart from extreme cases such as texts written in the Gulag.

Is writing work after all, and, in fact, less "intellectual" (a doubtful use of the concept "work") than physical? Does a writer not have to set ordinary hands, teeth, and licking tongue in motion at his work, and not just elegant fingertips?

Suddenly the informatic revolution looks like a solution. For in considering the tables shown in advertisements for so-called office supplies—these white, clean laboratory tables with their paper-free apparatuses, with smiling, elegant girls sitting at them—and comparing them with the desks of one's own experience, one appears to be a dinosaur wallowing about in the Triassic slime. It is the smiling girls, not I, who work with the "intellect" in the advertisements. The writer sitting at a desk is the material resistance against which they flutter. The girls are the ones who are really manipulating software, and they are more intellectual than we are.

As soon as we turn our attention back from the means to the text, of course, as soon as we disregard the stuff justifiably called "stupid," we are again caught up in a feeling of what's called the "will to the power of the pen." Only a bitter aftertaste has crept into the feeling. The stuff we are now disregarding really is stupid, but we have seen intelligent desks in the advertisements. Perhaps writing inspires us because our desks are so stupid? So as they become cleverer, do we writers become stupider? This existential question, arising at the office supply store and growing more insistent at the desk, will accompany all our writing from now on. It shows in our texts and can no longer be silenced. Once its doubtful position becomes clear, the desk in transition—standing, as Serre put it, at the "Northwest Passage"—will not be able to sustain itself. Its four legs wobble in the earthquake. The poor creature cannot be saved.

A summarizing look at stationeries and desks permits us to grasp the demise of writing as the demise of politics. Like all shops and exhibitions, stationeries show that the city and the public sphere (the space of publication) are doomed to disappear. Stationeries show in particular how the disappearance of paper marks the ends of trade. Desks, for their part, show how the power of the pen encounters no resistance and so can no longer realize itself, and the concept of power as such is displaced by a new concept of an automatically governed functioning so that all political thinking (a thinking in categories of power) bypasses the postliterate situation. A summarizing view of stationers and desks recognizes any political engagement by writers to be a ridiculous error. And so for most contemporary writers, such a perspective is not to be recommended, a perspective that further reveals another version of the known mismatch between means and ends. Throughout the whole of literary culture, the means were small and unimportant, and the ends were large and noble. It would be ridiculous to take Dante's goose quill into account in judging the purpose of the *Divine Comedy*. In this case, the means have without a doubt been redeemed by the result. But things have changed. Looking at the extraordinarily complex means assembled at an intelligent desk, and comparing them with the purposes they apparently serve, one might speak of the exact opposite—a redemption of the ends by the means. A visit to the stationer's alone shows that the stuff on offer is more splendid than the notes to be written, than what it is presumed to serve: how much more intelligence is embedded in such stuff than in the scribbling it is used to produce. The means have become so clever that they make the ends superfluous. They become their own purpose. Means becoming their own ends and ends become superfluous: this is what is meant by "media culture." That can be seen with exceptional clarity in thermonuclear armaments: the means are so powerful that any question about the ends borders on the stupid.

Attention has, finally, been focused on the means of writing. Entirely in keeping with the spirit of the times, it has neglected the purpose of writing. Is the question "to what purpose?" still meaningful, when constructed lines are giving way to puzzles made of particles?

Scripts

In recent years, there have been texts that are not directed to a publisher, and through him to readers, but rather to producers of film, television, and radio, and through these to viewers and listeners. People who write these texts are called "scriptwriters," a word that etymologically means something like "writing etcher," but no contemporary German equivalent occurs to me. This chapter empathizes with these people. It is not easy, for these people stand on slippery ground. It lies on a steep grade that forms a bridge between the uplands of literary culture and the abyss of the culture of technical images. So scriptwriters are always slipping, about to tumble head over heels into the abyss. Like tightrope walkers, they try to maintain a balance between text and image (text and sound) by means of literary acrobatics. But they can't do it because of the gravitational pull of the images. At least this circus act is not a public spectacle, for it occurs within the media and can only be taken in (read out) from media outputs (their programs). If scripts were public circus acts (if scriptwriters were to confront the public in the coliseum of the media), their reputation would spread far and wide. It would fill the space of the departing literary culture like a piercing scream: morituri te salutant.

A script is a hybrid: half of it is still a text for a drama to be staged, and so in the lineage of Sophocles, the other half is already the programming of apparatuses and as such an ancestor of programs calculated automatically by artificial intelligences. From the standpoint of the past, the scriptwriter is the playwright, from the standpoint of the future, a not quite fully automated word processor.

But like any chimera, the scriptwriter also has a life of his own, however ephemeral and ghostly. It is an injustice to see him as an informaticized Sophocles or as a tightrope walker. To empathize with him, one must try to put oneself in his position.

Radio scripts should be distinguished from all others right from the start. For while all the others are aimed at speaking images, the radio script aims at a speaker without images. Earlier in this essay, a claim was made that in the future, all sound of whatever sort will rush toward images. This would make radio, records, and tapes crippled communications media, amputated from images and able to preserve and reproduce themselves only because they are temporarily cheaper than comparable audiovisual media. This claim is vulnerable, for hasn't radio asserted itself in the face of the explosion in television and conquered a niche of its own in the structure of the media? Only the current inflation in portable radios, hi-fi systems, and Walkmans is probably little more than a passing anomaly. Once images are small enough to be built into armbands, and the sounds they emit are plastic enough to override the other oscillations that reach the ears, then imageless messages will prove to be an unnecessary impoverishment. No very bright future can be predicted for the writer of radio scripts.

That is regrettable, as he still is, after all, the closest of all script-writers to the playwright. As with Shakespeare, these are his own words that are being sent into space, and as with Shakespeare, a listener taken by the broadcast will read his text. These similarities certainly have limits. One can read the text of *Macbeth* before, after, or entirely independently of a theater production and each time receive a different message. One reads beforehand to visualize the drama. One reads afterward to determine how much of the text was lost in the drama and how much was added. One reads independently to dedramatize the text. In those rare cases when one reads a radio script, there is always an awkward feeling of having torn the text out of context, out of the context of a broadcast and out of that of the whole radio station. The text does not stand on its own two feet. Should it be complete in itself, it would be a bad script, one that does not fulfill the requirements the station set for it. Such a comparison of a script to a dramaturgical text shows a more profound change in orientation. We don't live dramatically anymore; rather we live programmatically.

Dramas show actions; programs give instructions about how to behave. Even those dramas that portray the greatest suffering (e.g., passion plays) seek to arouse sympathy and fear in us, that is, motivations for action. Programs enhanced by the most diverse array of actions awaken sensations, feelings, suffering in us, so that we will allow them to stimulate us. A dramatic orientation depends on a belief in the uniqueness, the indelibility of every action, that every past action is definitively past. It is the orientation of historical consciousness. A programmatic orientation rests on the belief in the eternal return of the same, on the indifference of every action. Programs actually reinforce this belief continually. It is the orientation of posthistorical consciousness.

However closely a scriptwriter for radio may resemble a playwright, he writes from a programmatic orientation. This (and not the coming crisis in radio) is the reason his future is not bright: he writes in an undramatic way when writing is a dramatic gesture. In writing his scripts, he contradicts himself. He is the victim of a particularly pernicious negative dialectic.

Other kinds of scripts present a far clearer case than does the chimera of the radio script. These are no longer texts; they are pretexts. This concept takes on its full meaning here: the sense of "pretence–betrayal" as well as that of "preliminary text." These scripts are lines of letters that are to be recoded into images. With them, the alphabet becomes an auxiliary code for making images. At the end of literary culture, the alphabet turns into its opposite. Having come from images to master them, it now turns back to them to fabricate them. Seen as a single, three-thousand-year passage, the whole of literary culture looks like a loop that runs out from images and back into them.

Literary texts that have been degraded to pretexts for images can be no more than a passing phenomenon. Scripts are written because, for the moment, there is all manner of alphabetically calibrated equipment lying around, that is, typewriters, word processors, and brains that store things alphabetically. Only spendthrifts would leave all this unused. As horse-drawn carriages became more rare and automobiles more common at the turn of the century, so will such devices become more rare and those calibrated to new codes more common in the near future. Very soon, there will be no further need to approach images in horse-drawn carriages, and scripts will give way to more functionally coded image instructions. Scripts are therefore a double pretence: they pretend to be texts while they are actually image programs; and they pretend that the alphabet is still functioning in image culture when, in fact, they are only using up a raw overstock of alphabet at the last minute, before the whole thing vanishes.

Scripts are the swansong of texts: a melancholy farewell from literature and, with it, from history in the exact sense of the word. The essential thing about texts is that they are aimed at a reader. Scripts no longer are. What is essential about texts, their hard core, has escaped from scripts. Only misty ghosts of texts remain, hovering about the grave of literature at the darkest hour of literary culture, before the morning wind of the rising informatic culture clears them from the air.

This is the way lines of letters look in their final stage, those letters that in their initial stage drove us in the direction of history: torn rags of lines with gaping holes in between. Discursive, critical thinking keeps starting again in them and keeps being brutally interrupted by emerging images. The long discourse that was inhaled with the first texts is now out of breath. One can speak of a telegraphic style and in so doing discover a unique beauty, namely, that of summary. But the staccato structure of this way of writing, as attractive as it may seem, is still only a pretext, a testimony to the new digital codes. The ideal of the gesture of writing is a legato, that binding of distinct elements into lines. Scripts abandon this ideal as unattainable. In abandoning the ideal of writing as a result of recognizing it to be unattainable, one has abandoned writing completely. Under the pretence that one can write in the reverse direction, toward a staccato, namely, in the direction of calculation and computing, scripts are written anyway. That is gruesome because only spineless things can tolerate that kind of distortion, distortion aimed at turning discursive, critical thought back into uncritical contemplation.

The ideal that writing set for itself is indeed unattainable. There is no legato. No one can glide, and even more definitely not since finding out that everything is made up of waves and droplets. It was necessary to *quantify* long before the term was invented. Scientific texts have not been alphabetic for a long time. They are alphanumeric and are becoming more numeric and less alphabetic all the time.

Writing equations is completely different from writing scripts. When I write algorithms, I am at one of the alphabet's boundaries, trying to cross this boundary in the direction of critical thinking. When I write scripts, I am putting critical thought into the service of images to be contemplated uncritically. It amounts to a swindle of discursive thought, a betrayal of the spirit of writing. Exactly because it is impossible to avoid the superficial similarity between mathematical codes and the new codes, the fundamental difference in intention must be pointed out. Numeric code intentionally promotes the alphabet ahead of itself; digital code intends to overthrow the alphabet. Scripts write in the way of digital codes.

Scripts are the way writers leave the sinking ship. That should be understood formally and existentially. One who writes scripts is committed body and soul to the culture of images, from the standpoint of literary culture, to the devil. Scriptwriters literally serve this devil. They put letters at his disposal. They tear letters from the sinking literary ship and offer them to the image devil. They submit to it in the true sense of the word—which means to accommodate and comply. It is doubtful that the philosopher Julien Benda was referring to such submission with the phrase "the betrayal of the intellectuals," but it might have occurred to him, had he seen contemporary film and television programming. No other betrayal of writers, of intellectuals, of the spirit of history is so clear as the one that scriptwriters commit. The results of this betrayal can be seen everywhere.

Linear history flows, channeled through scripts, into images, to revolve in them, according to program, in an eternal return of the same. That is the true reason that some scripts are called *Drehbücher* (turning books). These are books whose lines will be turned into circles. Such turning is possible because there are apparatuses behind the books that surround the lines, recoding them into images. In this way, history, which arose from images three thousand years ago, flows through the capillary vessels of scripts back into images. The unnatural thing about it is that the flow of history is accelerated in the process. The apparatuses suck history more and more greedily into themselves by way of scripts. They fall over one another to get into the whirling images. Never has history advanced so breathlessly as it has since the invention of image-making apparatuses, for at last, history has a concrete goal toward which to flow, namely, transformation into an image. All events occur with the increasingly clear purpose of being transformed.

So scriptwriters stand at the end of history and the beginning of apparatuses. They accelerate the output of history to provide the apparatuses with the necessary input. They deliver history to apparatuses and, in doing so, transmit to them the sense of everything that has happened. This sense is supposedly conveyed by the images. What they are doing is a horrible betrayal of history. The only reason we don't feel it daily and nightly is that in watching television and film, we have already lost historical consciousness. Scriptwriters, these gladiators of the media circus, catching writing in nets so as to strangle it and to themselves be strangled by it, arouse no anger in us because we who have become unconscious and impotent cannot even perceive them behind the images. We aren't aware of what the alphabet is still doing for images. In this very crucial sense, we have already become illiterate.

While we are staring at a few images lightly illuminated by the setting sun of the alphabet, something new is rising behind our backs whose first beams are already touching our surroundings. Like the slaves in Plato's cave, we must turn around to defy this newcomer.

The Digital

Among the perspectives available for gaining insight into the way things are being reordered, science holds a special position. Since the nineteenth century at the latest, natural science has been among the very few authorities that remain to us: we accept its conclusions without being forced by any kind of executive power. From the beginning of the twentieth century, it has been saying things so new that we haven't yet begun to digest them. As varied as these new things may be, they may be grasped in two watchwords: *relativity* and *quanta.*

The first watchword means that space, once seen as absolute, and time, once seen as clearly elapsing, are nothing more than relationships between observers, which is to say, subjects. And so spacing, the interval, becomes the key issue in epistemology and, in the near future, in perception, feeling, desire, and behavior.

The second watchword means that the world, once seen as solid, is no more than a swarm of tiny particles whirling about at random. And so probability and statistics have become the mathematics best suited to this world. Causes and effects appear only as statistical probabilities. Of course, that revolutionizes our feelings, desires, and behavior. We cannot continue to live as we did before.

The new assertions are hardly theoretical propositions only, to be discussed at leisure; rather they have had a practical effect. They have begun to reshape our lives from the ground up. One has only to recite the words *atomic power station, thermonuclear armaments, artificial intelligence, automation,* and *electronic information revolution.* It means that we have to grapple existentially with the new formulations daily and hourly. They have a practical orientation and open horizons of freedom and creative potential we had never suspected; on the other hand, they put our mental and physical endurance at risk. The new theoretical formulations of quantum theory are finding practical applications in technology faster than those of relativity theory. This is not to say that we should expect no astonishing practical effect from relativity theory. One has only to think of space travel. But it is to say that at present, we need to devote our full attention to problems raised by quanta. Far from being solely practical or epistemological issues, these are existential, political, and aesthetic ones. They should not be left to scientists and technicians.

In the meantime, what we once called "matter" (without quite knowing what we meant) has proven to be an affair of multiple levels. As bodies, we inhabit one level alone: that of molecules. Below this lie layers of atoms, nuclei, hadrons, and quarks, and above it are galaxies and black holes. How these levels relate to one another is an open question. Perhaps they are Russian dolls, with each doll contained by a higher one and containing a lower one, so that the astronomical universe is only a part of a previously unrecognized superuniverse—and the quark contains universes we've never suspected. Maybe it is about folds lying over folds, about wrinkles in wrinkles in wrinkles. It is in any case a lost cause to try to picture this. The crucial thing for this context is that we have discovered the following: as bodies, we inhabit the molecular level, but as thinking beings, we inhabit the level of the hadrons. Although its implications are inconceivable, this discovery already has practical applications.

Each single level has an appropriate structure. The astronomical one is Einsteinian; the molecular one is Newtonian; matter and energy swim in the atomic one; causality comes to an end in the nuclear one; the hadronic one requires a new mathematics and logic; with quarks, it makes no sense to distinguish between reality and symbol.

The boundaries between the levels blur. Astronautics goes

from molecules to the stars; chemistry from molecules to atoms; particle physics from molecules past atoms to nuclei. But so far, all of them have started their journeys at molecules. That will change. Once we understand the structure of our thinking better, we will travel from the hadrons (and the leptons and gluons) to the level of molecules. We will see the world of molecules, concrete things, animals, houses, human bodies from "below"—know it from there and act from there. Using a method chemistry knew nothing about and genetics only dimly suspected, we will be able to fabricate molecular material (living and nonliving beings).

We are in debt to neurophysiology for the knowledge that thinking is a process involving electrons, protons, and similar particles. It has shown that such particles jump across intervals in the astronomical numbers of nerve synapses that constitute the brain. What we call an idea, a feeling, a wish, or a decision turns out to be a statistical summary of quantum leaps; what we call perception turns out to be a summarizing of quantum leaps into a representation. In the brain, representations are formed from distinct elements, and from these in turn spring (in quanta) ideas, desires, feelings, and decisions. Given the nearly unbelievable complexity of the brain, the detail of how this happens is incomprehensible, but a simplified form of it can be simulated in thinking machines, so this understanding of thought is pragmatically "correct."

The level where thinking occurs is inconvenient for us in two ways. First, it can't be observed without the observation affecting what is being observed, so there can be no thought of objectivity in the sense of an object without a subject. Second, this is the realm of pure chance, which can be statistically ordered into curves but where it makes no sense to try to predict the future behavior of any one particle. In other words, everything that is possible, even the most improbable things, must eventually occur there. This slipperiness (it is impossible to grasp the object) and unpredictability (anything at all possible will at some point become necessary) are therefore characteristic of thinking. It can be steered, to be sure. Not only uncertainty and probability but also cybernetics is the appropriate discipline for thinking—which reminds us that cybernetic control itself comes from the level of uncertainty and statistical probability. This dizzying circle shows that we are beginning to reflect in a disciplined way for the first time, that is, to think about thinking.

From this incipient reflection on thinking has come, among other things and above all of them, the informatic revolution. It is a revolution because it turns from its point of departure to the world and to human beings. It no longer starts from solid things (from molecules) but rather from particles like electrons and protons, that is, at the level of thinking. Because it comes from below, it can change solid things, including human beings as bodies, more radically than any previous revolution—to say nothing of the changes it brings to humans as thinking beings. Although this revolution has only begun, it is possible to see a few of its fundamental features already. For example, it enables us to recognize solid objects as mere appearance, not just philosophically, but technically, inevitably making the world of such things less interesting. It further enables us to see particles on a screen, to compute them into images there, inevitably making the world of these particles increasingly more interesting. Third, it enables us to produce machines that think and work automatically, relying on articulated leaps of particles, demanding a reordering of all values bound up with work and thought. And finally, it enables us to analyze and synthesize thought processes from a new point of view, namely, that of informatics, and so we must learn to think differently.

At least two things characterize this relearning of thought: first, that we think images and only images, for everything we called perceptions—whether external or internal—are nothing but images computed in the brain; second, that thinking is not a continuous, discursive process—thinking "quantizes." That is an insight diametrically opposed to the concept of thinking that distinguishes Western culture. For us, thinking was, and still is, a process that moves forward, that frees itself from images, from representations, that criticizes them, thereby becoming increasingly conceptual. We have the alphabet to thank for this understanding of thought and this understanding of thought to thank for the alphabet (feedback). The new digital codes arose from the new understanding of thought, and feedback is making us think in quanta and images more clearly the more we use the new codes.

The quantum structure of the new codes will be treated here in isolation from its image-making function, although structure and function are obviously coordinated. The linear structure of the alphabet, too, can be thought independently of its function in writing stories, although structure and function are mutually conditional. Because of the particular construction of the apparatuses for which they are designed and that are supposed to decode them, the new codes are digital—and, in fact, usually binary, of the type 1–0. We are dealing with apparatuses that—like the telegraph—either let streams of electrons through (1) or interrupt them (0). Basically, all the new codes are supposed to do is give this mechanical turning on and off of the stream a meaning, to codify it (as flagging code lends meaning to the lifting and lowering of arms).

Apparatuses incorporate the 1–0 structure because they simulate the structure of our nervous system. There, too, we are dealing with a mechanical (and chemical) turning on and off of streams of electrons between the nerve synapses. From this standpoint, digital codes are a method—the first since human beings began to codify—of giving meaning to quantum leaps in the brain from the outside. We are faced with a self-concealing loop. The brain is an apparatus that lends meaning to the quantum leaps that occur in it, and now it is about to turn this meaning-giving function over to apparatuses of its own accord, then to reabsorb what they project. So the new codes are digital basically because they are using simulated brains to simulate the meaning-giving function of the brain.

This codification is an extraordinarily fast addition and subtraction of particulate impulses. It need not be linear, that is, in the form 1 + 1 + 1. It can proceed in multiple dimensions. The particulate impulses can be added and subtracted into surfaces, for example, so that strange images made of particles appear. This can be called "computing," for the particles can be so tightly compressed, com-puted, that their mosaic structure disappears from view. Something similar happens in the brain, and the images computed there are called "representations." The apparatuses simulate this brain function. What we see on their screens are simulated representations, whether they are images of objects in the world (houses, trees, people) or images of internal brain processes (equations, projections, fantasies, intentions, desires). From the images themselves, it is impossible to determine whether they represent external things (putative reality) or internal (putative fiction) ones. But that cannot be determined from brain representations either. Projecting brain function onto apparatuses raises exactly this question, whether this ontological distinction between real and fictional—this critique of images—is possible at all, and if it is possible, whether it is meaningful.

Simulation is a kind of caricature: it simplifies what is being imitated and exaggerates a few aspects of it. A lever is a simulation of an arm in that it neglects all aspects of an arm except the lifting function, but because it exaggerates this one function to such an extreme, it lifts much more effectively than the arm it is simulating. Thinking that expresses itself and makes images in digital codes is a caricature of thinking. But it is practically a public danger to underestimate this new way of thinking as somehow stupid or even narrow. The lever was the first caricature of the body's muscular function. By way of the Industrial Revolution, it led to mechanisms that have eliminated the muscular function of the human body from most areas. With regard to the simulation of thinking, we are at the high end of the lever. We are just beginning to learn, in the sense of projecting brain processes outward, so as to be able to free them from psychological, philosophical, and theological ideologies and get them going to full capacity. It is not that those who hold this new caricature of thought in ideological contempt can keep thought from emerging from its cranial cover, but they can make the path to free thought, laborious in itself, even more difficult. So critics and pundits nourished on alphabetic, historic thinking paradoxically become obstacles to the effort to free thinking from its physiological condition.

As the alphabet originally advanced against pictograms, digital codes today advance against letters to overtake them. As once, thinking that depended on the alphabet actively opposed magic and myth (pictorial thought), thinking that depends on digital codes is today actively engaged against process-oriented, "progressive" ideologies, replacing them with structural, systems-analytic, cybernetic ways of thinking. And as images defended themselves from history, from being strangled by texts, the alphabet is setting up its defenses at present so as not to be strangled by the new codes—only a small consolation to all those who continue their engagement with writing texts, for the whole thing has been accelerating. Only in the eighteenth century, after a three-thousand-year struggle, did texts succeed in pushing images, with their magic and myth, into such corners as museums and the unconscious. The current struggle won't take so long. Digital thinking will triumph much more quickly. It is true that the twentieth century is marked by a reactionary revolt of images. Should we anticipate a reactionary revolt of repressed texts against computer programs in an unpredictable future?

Recoding

We will have to relearn many things. That is difficult because what we have to learn is hard to acquire but, above all, because that which has once been learned is hard to forget. One advantage of artificial intelligences is that they have no difficulty forgetting. From them, we are learning the importance of forgetting. It is a tremendous thing to relearn, for it demands that we rethink the function of memory. In our tradition, memory is the seat of immortality: in Judaism, for example, one of life's goals is to remain in memory as a blessing. We must learn that it is just as important to be extinguished from memory. Death and immortality must be relearned, fame and anonymity must be revalued.

First among those things we must relearn in the context of the new as it emerges is process-oriented, progressive linear thought, the way of thinking that is articulated in linear writing. We will have to erase the alphabet from memory to be able to store the new codes there.

But might it be possible to learn the new codes without erasing what was stored in memory already? Isn't the brain a memory that is hardly used, that has a great deal of space available for new things, and is this not even more the case for those giant artificial memories we have begun to build? Doesn't the dialectic say that what has become obsolete is not lost but lifted up? Might it be that in the future, the new codes will be grounded in the alphabet, which they will assimilate into themselves and beyond, to new heights, so that rather than becoming illiterate, we become superliterate?

That is unthinkable. We will not be able to store the new codes over the alphabet in memory because these codes cannot tolerate the alphabet. They are impatiently imperialistic toward the alphabet. They cannot let a thought process geared toward criticizing images remain active behind their backs. The relationship between digital and alphabetic codes is no dialectic contradiction between image-producing and image-criticizing codes, capable of lifting each other to some sort of synthesis as it runs its course. It is rather about the formation of a new experience of space and time and so of a new concept of space and time into which the old experiences and concepts cannot go. This can no longer be grasped dialectically. Kuhn's concept of a "paradigm" works better: a sudden, previously unthinkable leap from one level to another rather than a synthesis from opposites. With digital codes, a new experience of time and space is emerging. Like a paradigm, it must obliterate everything that came before: all experiences that cannot yet be aligned under the old concepts of "omnipresence" and "simultaneity." Such experience cannot absorb but rather must destroy the alphabet.

Images produced with digital codes are present everywhere at the same time (even on the opposite ends of the earth). They can always be called into the present, even in an unthinkably distant future. Concepts of "present," "future," "past," and especially "distance" and "proximity" (i.e., "spacing") take on new meanings. The theory of relativity may well help us to acquire these new meanings, but we have to make them existential. In trying to do this, we are more impressed by the reversal of elapsing time than we are by the images' swallowing of space: no longer from the past toward the future but rather from the future toward the present. *Future* and *possibility* become synonyms, *time* becomes synonymous with "becoming more likely," and *present* becomes the realization of possibilities in form of images. *Future* turns into multidimensional compartments of possibilities that unravel outward toward the impossible and inward toward an image realized in the present. *Space* is just the topology of these compartments. Digital codes are a method of making these compartmentalized possibilities into images. Linear, historical, alphabetic thinking is incompetent for such a critique and must be eliminated.

There have been attempts to carry alphabetic thinking over into the digital and so to continue writing after all. There is the following argument, for example: it is in fact correct that linear thought, with its linear orthography (such as, say, Boolean logic or the historical consciousness of free will), cannot be reconciled with multidimensional and so quantized thought. But isn't linear, historical time, with its causality and concept of progress, one among the many dimensions in the new experience of time and space? When we experience the new images, don't we experience history, among other things? Can we not therefore say that the new experience of time (relative, phenomenological, cybernetic, and so on) and compression of space somehow does absorb the historical, the alphabetical into itself? These are decidedly modest attempts to secure a place for writing in the texture of a future culture.

They demonstrate how difficult it is to forget. For why should anyone want to describe what is coming, as this essay has been desperately trying to do? To want to describe it is to want to force it into the old thinking, to show how what is coming necessarily comes from the old, to explain it in terms of the old.

What is new about the new is its very indescribability, and that means that what is new about the new consists exactly in the absurdity of wanting to explain it. The Enlightenment has run its course, and there is nothing more to explain about the new. There is nothing obscure about it; it is as transparent as a net. There is nothing behind it. The Enlightenment has turned a somersault in the new. It must start to enlighten itself. The alphabet is the code of the Enlightenment. Writing can continue only with the goal of illuminating the alphabet, describing writing. Otherwise, there is nothing more to explain and describe.

Such a rescue attempt is concerned with the critical capacity of historical thought. Alphabetic thinking should not stop so that we can encounter the new images critically. But "criticism," too, must be relearned. In the old context, it means breaking what is to be criticized down into its elements. This is the way the alphabet criticizes images, for example, by breaking them up into pictoremes, then pixels, and then reordering them into lines. But the new images don't permit such criticism. They are synthetic, which is to say, they are assembled from previously isolated pixels. Digital codes synthesize things that have already been fully criticized, fully calculated. Criticism in the earlier sense could discover nothing more in these images than that they were computed from electrons. If this critique tried to go further and criticize the intentions of the synthesizer, it would, in the final analysis, find only computed electrons there as well. The old criticism, this dismantling of solid things, would be lost in the gaps between intervals, in nothingness—and to no purpose at all. For it is clear at the outset that there is nothing solid to be criticized in the new. A completely different critical method is required, one that is only approximately named by the concept "systems analysis." For this, alphabetic thinking is useless. This is not to say that we are surrendering to the new images uncritically; on the contrary, we will develop new methods so that we can analyze and resynthesize them. Such methods are already being developed. The attempt to rescue the old critical thinking may be noble, but it is completely beside the point.

We will have to learn to write digitally, should *writing* still be a suitable designation for such a means of notation, and should anyone still be able to see it as a recoding from old into new codes. One who regards digital codes as written codes and sees a continuity between them and prealphabetic image making and alphabetic text making could claim to need to learn to recode everything: not only everything written but also everything still to write. We will have to recode the whole of literature, the whole factual and imaginary library of our culture into digital codes to be able to feed them to artificial memories and call them down from there. We will have to recode everything still to be written, all those unfinished thought processes set out in texts, into digital codes. One who sees digital code as the articulation of a radically new way of thinking that can't be called writing, on the other hand, could say that we will be forced to erase the whole factual and imaginary library from memory, with all its achievements and all its unfinished beginnings, to clear a space for the new. But basically, these two formulations amount to the same thing: we will have to learn to rethink our entire history, backward and forward—a dizzying assignment after all.

How dizzying it all is becomes clear when we put ourselves in the position of a future reader. Let's assume that the world's literature has already been digitally recoded, stored in artificial memories, and its original alphabetic form erased. The future reader sits in front of the screen to call up the stored information. This is no longer a passive taking in (pecking) of information fragments along a prewritten line. This is more like an active accessing of the cross-connections among the available elements of information. It is the reader himself who actually produces the intended information from the stored information elements. To produce the information, the reader has various methods of access available, which are suggested to him by the artificial intelligence (methods currently called "menus"), but he can also apply his own criteria. And certainly we should expect a whole future science concerned with criteria for and links to bits of information (so-called documentation sciences are starting to do this). What happens in such reading can be seen more clearly in an example.

Let's assume that the reader is interested in the history of science, that is, in pieces of information that follow one another in a chronological order from the standpoint of the reader's present. According to our current ways of reading and thinking, "Aristotle" would, for example, come before "Newton." To the future reader, "Aristotle" and "Newton" are simultaneously accessible, both coded digitally. So he can access both systems at the same time, and in such a way that they overlap and disturb one another. In the Newton system, for example, "inertia" will run up against "motive" in the Aristotle system, and the principle of "justice" in Aristotle's system will bump into the chains of causality in Newton's system. The reader will be able to manipulate the two overlapping systems so that an intermediate stage emerges in which Aristotle's system could arise from Newton's as well as Newton's from Aristotle's. From the available data, the reader will find out that the Newtonian system is, in fact, more recent than the Aristotelian, but he can just as easily reverse the history.

The example was chosen to show that the future reader will be free to access linear, historical cross-links between elements of information among others. He will be able to read the history of science, among other things, from his data. But the history that comes from such a reading is precisely not what we mean by "history." Historical consciousness—this awareness of being immersed in a dramatic and irreversible flow of time—has vanished from the future reader. He is above it, able to access his own flow of time. He doesn't read along a line but rather spins his own nets.

Recoding literature into the new codes is a dizzying assignment. It demands that we translate our thought world into a foreign one: from the world of spoken languages into that of ideographic images, from the world of logical rules into that of mathematical ones, and above all, from the world of lines into that of particulate nets.

We probably will not be able to begin before we have developed a theory and philosophy of translation. We are very far from this. Still we can see recoding under way everywhere (although not yet, except in fantasy, the destruction of recoded texts).

In the recoding of texts into films, records, television programs, and computer images, what is happening to scientific texts is the most remarkable. Here statements that rest on logical and mathematical thought become images, and these images are colorful and mobile. This is the way scientific thought is translated into the new codes with no appropriate theory of translation available. Political and aesthetic risks, such as the filming of novels or the transposition of poetry to the television screen, pale by comparison to this epistemological danger.

In the matter of recoding, we face two opposing tendencies. On one hand we have people who don't want to learn to recode for they don't believe it is necessary to learn afresh. On the other hand, we have people who approach everything written and yet to be written with the intention of recoding it, either because they sense an adventure or simply because they have begun to be repulsed by all the scribbling. Between these two extremes are some who are simultaneously aware of both the necessity and the difficulty of recoding, that is, relearning. These are the people from whom a theory and philosophy of translation is to be expected. If it is achieved, the transition from the alphabetic into the new culture will become a conscious step beyond current conditions of thought and life. If it is not achieved, a descent into illiterate barbarism is to be feared.

One might object that everything has always been on a knife's edge without having actually fallen to either of the two sides—which leads to the conclusion that the proverbial edge is probably exceedingly dull. But isn't the feeling of a knife's edge exactly what is responsible for what we call "freedom"? Looking forward from here is the sharp knife, backward from here, inert porridge, and do we have to look forward? To those of us who spell things out, the current transition from the alphabet to the new looks like a dangerous step on a ridge between abysses. It may seem like a pleasant stroll to our grandchildren, but we are not our grandchildren, who will learn the new with ease in kindergarten. Do we have to go back to kindergarten?

Subscript

We have to go back to kindergarten. We have to get back to the level of those who have not yet learned to read and write. In this kindergarten, we will have to play infantile games with computers, plotters, and similar gadgets. We must use complex and refined apparatuses, the fruit of a thousand years of intellectual development, for childish purposes. It is a degradation to which we must submit. Young children who share the nursery with us will surpass us in the ease with which they handle the dumb and refined stuff. We try to conceal this reversal of the generation hierarchy with terminological gymnastics. While we're about this boorish nonsense, we don't call ourselves Luddite idiots but rather progressive computer artists. And we try to aggrandize ourselves, to ourselves and to others who go on writing and thinking by the old methods, by writing learned and lofty comments on our nonsense. But it can't fool anyone. What we're doing as we sit before our Minitels, Apples, and Commodores is so primitive that no symposia, workshops, or seminars can cover it up. It is just a caricature of thinking.

Our tradition has a ready vindication for this, our intentional relapse. Didn't Jesus suggest, for example, that should we wish to enter into the kingdom of heaven, we should become as little children? Only a consciousness that has been laboriously achieved and energetically defended is not quite so easy to get rid of. In Jesus's time, it was surely about undermining Greek art and science, Jewish theosophy, and casuistry so as to clear a space for naive faith. The result, as we know, was that strange mixture of the primitive, barbarous, and decadent we call the early Middle Ages. In hindsight, we do recognize the seeds of a splendid development in this mixture. It brought dismantled Greek thought forward as the Renaissance and dismantled Jewish thought as the Reformation. We don't have sufficient distance from contemporary crudity, barbarism, and decadence to be able to recognize seeds of splendor, however clearly we may sense them. It is not a principle of hope that propels us back to kindergarten but rather a principle of desperation, namely, the common persuasion: we can't go on like this.

So the curtain is falling on the stage where the drama of written culture, that struggle of the spirit against the powers of obscurantism, played itself out. In the course of this drama, there have been grim scenes: when the antagonist, perhaps in the form of national socialism, took center stage; when the protagonists themselves as, say, Inquisitors injured themselves horrifically. Such scenes cast doubts on any engagement with the departing culture. And still we are unable to take any lighthearted leave of this drama. It was a splendid show, and we are still taken by it. "I come to bury Caesar, not to praise him."

As people first began to write in that easterly corner of the Mediterranean more than three thousand years ago, the lifeworld was small compared to ours and was filled with obstacles. It was only a few human generations old, and there were people giving a firsthand account of its beginnings. The world's span was large, but one could still walk around it. To move anywhere in this circle was to bump into superhuman powers, extracting a terrible revenge on any who did not make sacrifices and prostitute themselves. These powers, antagonistic to human beings, surrounded people everywhere in the form of threatening images. Only rarely and reluctantly, then, did people leave the protective space of the village, that human segment of an inhuman lifeworld that had been culturally secured. Monsters lay in wait for those who left culture for adventure. A stranger coming into the village constituted an invasion of what was livable, familiar by something monstrous. People lived out their relatively few years in thrall to such communities.

When they died, it was murder, by human or superhuman hands, and that had to be avenged by the survivors.

Alphabetic lines broke through this narrow magical circle. They opened sweeping vistas. The origin of the world was pushed back far beyond the human scale, measurable only in such existentially meaningless terms as, say, fifteen billion years. The world's circumference expanded into the immeasurable and collapsed into the inconceivable. To move just far enough anywhere, whether in the enormous or the minute, is to encounter emptiness. Not only have we seen through the superhuman powers that condition us (and that is all four forces: gravitational, electromagnetic, "strong," and "weak"), we have in part enlisted them in our service. In this world that has become vast, empty, and in part serviceable, we move about with increasing speed and agility. As we do, we bump only into one another. We delay death as long as we can and then suppress or deny it. All these violent changes in the lifeworld, completely improbable three thousand years ago, are the result of alphabetic lines.

One might say that alphabetic lines and the thought that moves along them illuminated the stolid darkness of the magical–mythical lifeworld, that they cut windows in this world, letting the light of critical thought in. But that would not give the alphabetic reordering credit for its final consequences. It did begin to open windows, but later critical thinking also built doors people used to go out and experience the world. Finally, it tore down the walls. Today the clear light of critical thought floods the whole environment from all sides. Even the individual human being is illuminated in his innermost being with such cold X-rays. This means there is nothing left to illuminate. There is nothing to stop the rays of critical thinking. They run into a void.

With this, alphabetic writing and thinking have reached and exceeded their original goal. To think further, one would have to use new codes. But to maintain that linear consciousness has overshot its goal and is about to lose itself in nothingness is to practice historical critique and so linear thought after all, for it is to say that history is a process that led from the narrow abundance of prehistory to the open emptiness of posthistory.

The goal of historical consciousness is unattainable for this peculiar reason: only historical consciousness has goals (it is linear); other levels of consciousness do not. Therefore, in setting itself the goal of reaching a level of consciousness without goals, historical consciousness will come to a false conclusion. Goals can be pursued within history but not in mythology and not in the new. Only in this sense are we justified in saying the history has *over*-shot its goal: a new form of aimlessness has emerged from it. That is to say, history can go ahead and pursue its goals (which it can never achieve), but to the new consciousness, observing it all from above, it doesn't matter.

The level of consciousness that prevailed before history is articulated pictorially, the historical alphabetically, the new digitally. Abysses open between them. Each alphabetic attempt to bridge the abyss in the direction of the digital will fail because it will carry its own linear, goal-oriented structure into the digital, covering the digital up. So the alphabetic model of consciousness just proposed should be erased after use. The same is true of this entire alphabetic essay to the extent that it tries to write past writing. The provisional assistance it offers is to be applied to the new with justified mistrust and then erased.

Inasmuch as this essay has tried to write past writing, it is to be erased after use. Inasmuch as it has written about writing (and obviously not written far enough), it should be read as a subscript to writing—and this in a double sense: as confirmation of what has been written (underwriting) and as the last written thing before the end (signature).

The objection could be raised that writing does not need to be confirmed. Surely it is presumptuous of a writer to except himself from wanting to underwrite this ancient and splendid articulation of the spirit with his own name. But is it not common today for petitions and protests to circulate to collect thousands of signatures? This essay, this subscript, wants to be read as one among thousands, one underwriting of a petition in support of a writing that stands accused, one signature on a protest against the threat of secondary illiteracy, even as stifled tears. But how can the tears be completely stifled when writing is being carried to its grave, even if, at some level of consciousness a hair's breadth thick, tears seem inappropriate?

The last writing—that's ridiculous, some will say. Certainly more tides of writing will flow through the presses and technically advanced reproduction apparatuses and into the environment. The writer of this essay will, with certainty bordering on probability, write more: he cannot do otherwise. And in light of such text inflation, it does make sense, in the final analysis, to call them all last writings. The present essay has tried to suggest this.

There are people who write because they think it still makes sense, and there are people who no longer write but go back to kindergarten. And then there are people who write despite knowing that it makes no sense. This essay is actually directed at the first two but dedicated to the third.

Afterword to the Second Edition

New editions should really consider the old ones, and the new considerations should supplement the old. This supplemental text will not need to be so concerned with bringing things up to date because the text is an essay. An essay is an attempt to stimulate others to reconsider, to move them to provide supplements. That is the reason this text is also to be published as a disk: it is intended to be a snowball, the initial presentation increasingly covered over by subsequent additions. A series of branching new editions should unfold, with new considerations overlapping the earlier ones. Publishing an essay is not about proving or disproving something (as in an experiment) but about constantly rethinking everything dialogically. That there is a new edition proves that we're still concerned with writing and not with what comes after writing. It is just not so easy to break out of writing and into afterthoughts. The essay's lack of success in this respect is to be taken into consideration.

The text suggests that there are fundamentally just two ways out of writing: back to images or forward to numbers; back to the imagination or forward into calculation. In the course of these considerations, it turned out that these two directions could surreptitiously merge: numbers may be computed into images. One could try to break out of textual, writing-based thought into intuitive calculations. If this were to succeed, it would lift both calculating and imaginative thinking into the textual. Writers would then have swallowed mathematicians and image makers, digested them, and in so doing raised themselves to a new level. It didn't work here.

Regrettably, the explanation is simple: the one making the attempt was a writer whose mathematical competence is inadequate. One might think one could have known that beforehand. But in fact, those whose mathematical competence is sufficient don't try to break out of writing, for they have already set it aside in contempt. So the attempt must be made despite being aware of one's own incompetence (of inevitable failure). That is just what is dramatic about essayistic thinking: it knows its own incompetence and turns to those with greater competence to continue to try.

Knowing one's own incompetence is not necessarily a disadvantage. It is possible to laugh at oneself in the process to keep the effort moving forward. So not *ridendo castigat mores* but *ridendo castigat se ipsum.* And this was perhaps not a complete failure after all, for it could lead to the second edition we have before us now.

V. F., June 1989

Translator's Afterword and Acknowledgments

Nancy Ann Roth

Vilém Flusser, like Walter Benjamin, understood translation as an engagement with language as such, resonating far beyond the fortunes of any particular text. But where Benjamin's thought seemed to move toward a convergence among languages, a point where "the original and the translation [become] recognizable as fragments of a greater language,"[1] Flusser was keenly conscious of moments and spaces between codes, leaps between standpoints. He speaks of intractable antagonisms between certain kinds of codes, notably between images and linear texts, or more exactly, between the magical and historical consciousnesses they respectively support. He describes codes locked in combat as the historical subjects of triumph or defeat.

Flusser spoke five languages, wrote for publication in four of them, and knew enough of several more to draw on them for quotations and etymological evidence. But as he made clear in an essay called "The Gesture of Writing," he did not experience the languages stored in his memory as equal in the sense that all would cover the same ground or all be simultaneously available to express a particular thought. In a passage in the present book, in fact, he differentiates among the spoken languages he knows by their various ways of resisting his effort to force them into lines of writing: "Each language defends itself according to its character," he writes. "German is slippery, English brittle, French deceptive, Portuguese sly."

In "The Gesture of Writing," Flusser describes what must be a unique pattern of translating his own texts into other languages and, sometimes, back again into the original. That particular essay exists in seven different versions in four different languages.[2] Nor is it coincidence that the most comprehensive study of Flusser's work to date, Rainer Guldin's 2005 *Philosophieren zwischen den Sprachen (Philosophizing between Languages),*[3] is organized around the concept of translation.

This is not, could not, be a "true" translation by Flusser's standards ("I believe that the only true translation is the one attempted by the author of the text to be translated").[4] And yet perhaps exactly because he was so conscious of distinctions, frictions among codes, he was also sensitive to a limit, to the possibility of a gap too wide to jump, of codes so different that no translation is possible. In the afterword to the second edition, he quite explicitly confesses to having himself failed to achieve a true translation of the kind most urgently needed now, namely, a recoding from alphanumeric texts into algorithmic code—into technical images. He shares his sense of despair, first at his own incapacity to be the author of such a translation, and then at the failure of his book to have finally transcended its own status as a book, to attract the kinds of translators who might have recoded it for an emerging consciousness.

This book remains a book, addressed to readers, and not an algorithm for sound and image. And because it is a book and because we are still readers, it bears witness to the currency of his thought. I can say, now, in English, "I wrote it nevertheless."

I'll always be grateful to Anke Finger for her instant enthusiasm when I first told her I wanted to translate Flusser's work into English. She, as well as Andreas Ströhl and Rainer Guldin, have been reliably generous with their support at all points. I am grateful to Lambert Wiesing, a philosopher with both a high professional regard and an infectious enthusiasm for Flusser's work, who offered his general encouragement and specific advice about an English translation. Marcel Marburger kindly shared both his knowledge of pertinent materials in the Flusser-Archiv in Berlin and my concern about English equivalents for a few crucial words with unique resonances in German. For all of us, Edith Flusser continues to be an inspiration, a person of enormous warmth and energy, always eager to foster creative dialogue about her husband's work.

I'd like to thank Doug Armato, Adam Brunner, and Danielle Kasprzak at the University of Minnesota Press, for their kindness to me and their commitment to making more of Flusser's work available in English, and Andreas Müller-Pohle, this book's first publisher, for his support of this English edition. It is, finally, most fortunate that my husband, Michael Whetman, is an artist who reads voraciously and likes to talk about words. Beyond this, however, he is essential to creating an immediate reality in which I am able to translate books.

Translator's Notes

Superscript

1   The German chapter title is "Überschrift," meaning either "above" or "about" writing and also having the sense of a title or heading.

Letters of the Alphabet

1   *Buchstaben* is an archaic way of forming the plural.

Poetry

1   *Communicology (Kommunikologie)* is Flusser's term for his own field of study, the study of communication.

Books

1   The publisher and translator of this book did want an index.

Letters

1   PTT (Postes, télégraphes et téléphones) administrated postal services and telecommunications in France from 1921 until 1991, when it was split into La Poste and France Télécom.

Translator's Afterword

1   Walter Benjamin, "The Task of the Translator," in *Illuminations* (New York: Schocken, 1969), 78.

2   Rainer Guldin, *Philosophieren zwischen den Sprachen: Vilém Flussers Werk* (Munich: Wilhelm Fink, 2005), 280.

3   Ibid.

4   Vilém Flusser, "The Gesture of Writing," unpublished typescript in original English, p. 11.

Index

algorithm: at the alphabet's boundary, 137; not recognized by art critics, 24–25; as picture, 24

alphabet: as antidote to pictorial thinking, 31, 32, 147; as auxiliary code for making images, 135; deferred to by numeric code, 137; digital code's incompatibility with the, 137, 149–50; as dominant code, 63; effect on spoken language, 33–34, 63–64, 67; as expression of Western thought, 53; future loss of the, 30, 31, 35, 42, 75, 77, 139, 159, 160; invention of, 30, 34–35; in relation to numbers, 31; link between poetry and the, 71–72, 74–76; as obstruction to digital codes, 147, 149–51, 160; perceived need for more than one, 50; in relation to binary code, 55–56; rendered superfluous through informatics, 53, 63; as signs for sound, 24, 31; survival of, 151–52

alphanumeric code. *See* code, alphanumeric

Anti-Oedipus (Deleuze and Guattari), xxi

apparatuses: advantages over human beings, 58–59; binary code for, 145; decision-making in the service of, 115; future replacement of publishers by, 42; turning history into images, 138; as writers of history, 21; poetry in the context of, 71–72, 74; programmed to simulate brain function, 146; programming as writing for, 55, 56

art: concept that blocks access to new images, 28–29; computer, 60, 109; convergence with science, 29, 83; decline in, 105; inadequacy of term in relation to computer images, 28

Bacon, Francis, x
Baudrillard, Jean, xi
Benda, Julian, 138
Benjamin, Walter, 28
Betrayal of the Intellectuals (Benda), 138

Vilém Flusser (1920–91) was born in Prague; emigrated to Brazil, where he taught philosophy and wrote a daily newspaper column in São Paulo; and later moved to France. He wrote several books in Portuguese and German. In addition to the University of Minnesota Press's *Writings* volume (2004) and *Into the Universe of Technical Images* (Minnesota, 2011), *The Shape of Things, Toward a Philosophy of Photography,* and *The Freedom of the Migrant* have been translated into English.

Mark Poster is professor of history at the University of California, Irvine. His books include *What's the Matter with the Internet?* (Minnesota, 2001), *The Second Media Age, The Mode of Information,* and *Cultural History and Postmodernity.*

Nancy Ann Roth is a writer and critic based in the United Kingdom. She was the translations editor for *German Expressionism: Documents from the End of the Wilhelmine Empire to the Rise of National Socialism,* edited by Rose-Carol Washton Long.